# 1000

## Questions & Answers
### about

Australia

*Steve Parish*
**DISCOVER & LEARN**
ABOUT AUSTRALIA

www.steveparish.com.au

# Introduction

## ABOUT 1000 Questions & Answers about Australia

EVERYONE enjoys solving puzzles, and Australia is a land full of mysteries, secrets and little-known facts.

This collection of questions should test your knowledge of Australia. It should also test your memory, your powers of observation and deduction, and your instinct for sources which will give you the information you need.

SOURCES FOR ANSWERS include *Steve Parish Publishing Amazing Facts Books 1-8* and the *Steve Parish Publishing Australia Guide*.

Some questions can be answered with the aid of an atlas or road maps of Australia.

For up-to-date statistics you could consult the Australian Bureau of Statistics site on the Internet. Other useful sources could be *The Little Aussie Fact Book*, compiled by Margaret Nicholas and published by Penguin Books, and *The Australian Almanac 2000* published by Hardie Grant Books.

Check out the pictures that illustrate the pages and the captions, as the answer can sometimes be discovered there.

THE ANSWERS to the questions begin on page 54. There is an Index to the subjects of illustrations on page 64.

KEEP A SCORE of your correct answers and try the questions on your friends. If you can answer more than 800 questions correctly, your knowledge of Australia is very good. If you score over 900, you have a future in games and quiz shows!

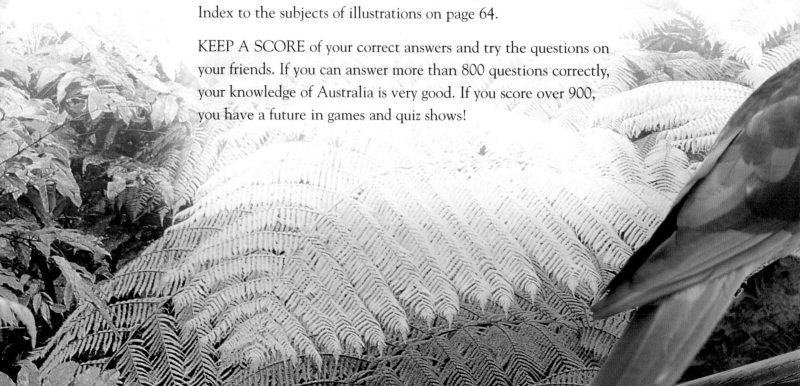

# Contents

Introduction                               2

## THE QUESTIONS

Australia – General                        4

New South Wales                            8

Victoria                                   12

Tasmania                                   16

South Australia                            19

Western Australia                          22

Northern Territory                         26

Queensland                                 30

Australian Capital Territory               34

Australia's Landforms                      37

Australia's Plants                         41

Australia's Animals                        44

Timeline Australia                         48

## THE ANSWERS                             54

Index to Illustrations                     64

**Q.1** What currency is used in Australia?

**Q.2** Are all Australian banknotes the same colour?

**Q.3** What Australian wildlife features on the reverse side of the 10 cent coin?

**Q.4** What are the colours of the Australian $10, $20 and $50 notes?

**Q.5** What is the nickname for Australia's interior: the Dieback, the Hardback, the Throwback, the Outback or the Lineback.

An Outback river

**Q.6** Do most Australians live in the interior or around the coast?

**Q.7** What is the population of Australia: about 17 million, about 18 million, about 19 million, about 20 million or about 21 million?

Superb Lyrebird

**Q.8** True or false? Around 22% of Australians were born overseas.

**Q.9** Australia is divided into six States and two Territories. Name them.

**Q.10** Where does Australia's Federal Parliament sit?

**Q.11** Is Australia a member of the British Commonwealth of Nations?

**Q.12** Who is the Head of State of Australia?

**Q.13** On what date did the Commonwealth of Australia come into being?

**Q.14** What Commission represents the interests of Aborigines and Torres Strait Islanders: ATYIC, ATSIG, ATSIC, ANSIC or ANZAC?

**Q.15** What does the name Australia mean?

**Q.16** Before 1788, did all Australian Aborigines speak the same language?

**Q.17** What do the following places have in common: Norfolk Island, Macquarie Island, the Cocos Islands, Christmas Island and Australian Antarctica?

**Q.18** What is the meaning of the term "indigenous Australian"?

**Q.19** True or false? Australia's States have their own parliaments.

**Q.20** Which two bodies make up most Australian State Parliaments?

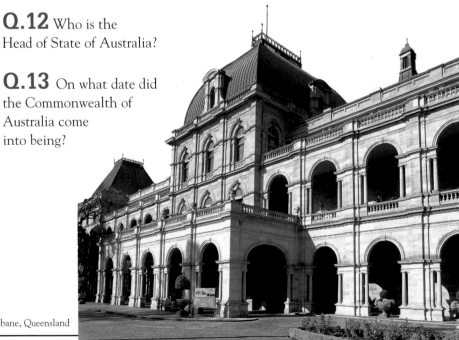
Parliament House, Brisbane, Queensland

Federal House of Representatives Chamber

The Australian flag

**Q.21** What title is given to the leader of the party holding most seats in the Federal House of Representatives?

**Q.22** What is the name for a member of the governing party who is responsible for a particular area: a backbencher, a minister, a prime mover, a manager or a principal?

**Q.23** True or false? The Australian Labor Party is the youngest Labor Party in the world.

**Q.24** Which Australian State was the first to allow women to vote?

**Q.25** What is the age at which Australians may vote?

**Q.26** How many stars appear on the Australian flag?

**Q.27** When is the Australian Flag flown at half-mast?

**Q.28** True or false? The Australian Flag should not be used as a seat cover, to cover a statue or as a carpet.

**Q.29** What are the colours of the Aboriginal Flag?

Golden Wattle

**Q.30** What do the three areas on the Aboriginal Flag represent?

**Q.31** Match daily newspapers and the cities in which they are published: *the Age, the Courier Mail, the Mercury, the West Australian*: Perth, Brisbane, Melbourne, Hobart.

**Q.32** What Australian spread made of yeast extract was once known as "Parwill"?

**Q.33** What is the first line of the Royal Anthem and when is it used in Australia?

**Q.34** What is Australia's National Anthem?

**Q.35** What is Australia's national floral emblem?

**Q.36** What do Edmund Barton, William Morris Hughes, Robert Menzies, John Curtin and Paul Keating have in common?

**Q.37** What is the document which lists the powers of the Federal Government called: the Restitution, the Reconciliation or the Constitution?

**Q.38** True or false? The Australian Constitution can be changed by a majority of YES votes in a minority of States.

**Q.39** Which native animals support Australia's Coat of Arms?

**Q.40** Is voting compulsory in State and Federal elections?

Australia's Coat of Arms

**Q.41** Is Australia in the Southern or the Northern Hemisphere?

**Q.42** Name the three oceans and one sea that between them surround Australia.

**Q.43** What is the stretch of water between Australia and Tasmania called: The Strait and Narrow, Bass Strait, Torres Strait, Tasman Strait or Dire Strait?

Viewing Australia's coastline

**Q.44** True or false? Australia's coastline, including Tasmania, measures 36 735 km.

**Q.45** Which is closest to Australia: Indonesia, Antarctica, Papua New Guinea or New Zealand?

**Q.46** What is the approximate area of Australia: 5 682 300 km², 6 682 300 km², 7 682 300 km² or 8 682 300 km²?

**Q.47** How many time zones are there within the Australian continent?

**Q.48** How many times would the British Isles fit into Australia: 8 times, 12 times, 16 times, 20 times or 24 times?

**Q.49** Which is the longer distance, across Australia north–south or east–west?

**Q.50** True or false? Australia is the wettest continent on earth.

**Q.51** Which Tropic passes through Australia: the Tropic of Capricorn or the Tropic of Cancer?

**Q.52** True or false? New South Wales, Victoria, Tasmania and Queensland observe Eastern Summer Time.

**Q.53** What natural feature off the coast of Queensland can be seen from space?

**Q.54** What town is nearest the centre of the Australian continent?

**Q.55** Australia's highest recorded temperature was at Cloncurry (Q) in 1889. Was it 49.1°C, 50.1°C, 51.1°C, 52.1°C or 53.1°C.

**Q.56** Where did the record low temperature of minus 23°C occur in 1994: Dunk Island, Thredbo, Charlotte Pass, Oodnadatta or Mt Wellington?

Part of the Great Barrier Reef

**Q.57** What is Australia's lowest point?

**Q.58** What is the name of the furthest north point of the Australian mainland?

**Q.59** What are El Niño and La Niña: mountains, ocean currents, cyclonic winds, the Mexican Ambassador's children or feral animals?

**Q.60** If El Niño occurs, will eastern Australia have a wet or a dry summer?

Cape York, Queensland

# Australia – General

Ubirr, Kakadu National Park, Northern Territory

**Q.61** Australia has twelve areas on the list of World Heritage Sites. Name two of them.

**Q.62** True or false? Up to 90% of Australia's rainfall may be lost through high rates of evaporation.

**Q.63** What do the following have in common: the Kelpie sheepdog, the billy, surf lifesaving clubs, the pavlova and indoor cricket?

**Q.64** True or false? Surfboard riding was invented in Australia.

**Q.65** True or false? The Western Plateau is a tableland which covers most of the eastern side of the Australian continent.

**Q.66** Which river forms the boundary between two Australian States?

**Q.67** Which Australian city staged the 2000 Olympic Games?

**Q.68** Which city would you expect to be warmer in winter, Melbourne or Darwin?

**Q.69** Rank the following State capitals in order of population size: Hobart, Brisbane, Melbourne, Sydney, Perth.

**Q.70** What city is Australia's Federal Capital?

**Q.71** What do the initials CSIRO stand for?

**Q.72** True or false? The highest mountains in Australia are in the arid central deserts?

Great Dividing Range, Victoria

Surf Lifesaving Carnival

**Q.73** Does most of the Great Dividing Range run north–south or east–west?

**Q.74** On which side of Australia is the Great Dividing Range?

**Q.75** Why is Darwin not a State Capital city?

**Q.76** What is Australia's largest city?

**Q.77** In what year was the first Melbourne Cup run, 1841, 1851, 1861, 1871 or 1881?

**Q.78** Which of these sporting personalities is not Australian: Sir Donald Bradman, Roy Cazaly, Greg Norman, Wayne Gardner, Michael Jordan?

**Q.79** True or false? Australia is one of only three countries to have taken part in every modern Olympic Games.

**Q.80** How did the following people make their living: Sidney Nolan, Norman Lindsay, Margaret Preston, Albert Namatjira and Tom Roberts?

Darwin, Northern Territory

**Q.81** True or false? New South Wales is Australia's largest State.

**Q.82** What is the area of New South Wales: 601 600 km², 801 600 km² or 1001 600 km²?

**Q.83** Is Lord Howe Island part of New South Wales?

**Q.84** Which other States border New South Wales?

**Q.90** What is the highest point of New South Wales? Mt Kilimanjaro, Mt Erebus, Mt Sturt, Mt Kosciuszko or Mt Isa?

**Q.91** What is the animal emblem of New South Wales?

**Q.92** Place these New South Wales cities in order of population size: Wollongong, Sydney, Broken Hill, Wagga Wagga, Newcastle.

**Q.93** When did the First Fleet arrive in New South Wales?

Platypus

**Q.94** Who made up the largest group on the First Fleet: marines, free settlers, sailors, convicts or officers?

**Q.95** Bennelong was an Aboriginal ambassador between his people and the British settlers. What Sydney building stands on ground named after him?

**Q.96** Who was the first Governor of New South Wales: Captain Arthur Phillip, Captain William Bligh, Captain James Cook or Captain Courageous?

Sydney Opera House

**Q.85** What is the name of the range of mountains which runs down the eastern side of New South Wales?

**Q.86** True or false? More than half the population of New South Wales live in the State's capital city, Melbourne.

**Q.87** What is the floral emblem of New South Wales?

**Q.88** How many people live in New South Wales: around 6 million, around 7 million or around 8 million?

**Q.89** Which two of the following animals hold up the shield on the New South Wales Coat of Arms? Emu, Red Deer, Lion, Aardvark, Thylacine, Kangaroo.

**Q.97** Who founded New South Wales's fine wool industry: John and Elizabeth Gould, John and Elizabeth Macarthur or John and Elizabeth Merino?

**Q.98** Which mountains west of Sydney did Blaxland, Wentworth and Lawson cross in 1813?

**Q.99** When was New South Wales separated from Victoria: 1820, 1830, 1840, 1850 or 1860?

Waratah

**Q.100** True or false? Sydney Harbour has over 300 km of shoreline.

**Q.101** What type of rock underlies Sydney: sandstone, limestone, greenstone, bloodstone or opalstone?

**Q.102** Royal National Park, near Sydney, was the world's first national park. When was it created: 1869, 1879, 1889, 1899 or 1909?

The Three Sisters

The AMP Tower at Centrepoint in Sydney

**Q.103** True or false? The Coat of Arms of Sydney includes a Rainbow Serpent.

**Q.104** What is the tallest building in Sydney?

**Q.105** True or false? Sydney is multicultural.

**Q.106** What is the name of Sydney's harbourside Zoo: Taringa, Taroonga, Taronga, Tarunga or Taranga?

**Q.107** What famous sporting event was held in Sydney in 2000: the Melbourne Cup, the Commonwealth Games, the Stawell Gift, the Olympic Games or the Americas Cup?

**Q.108** What building stands on Cape Byron?

**Q.109** In summer, why is Tweed Heads (NSW) one hour ahead of its adjoining town Coolangatta (Q)?

**Q.110** What political dividing line runs between Coolangatta and Tweed Heads?

**Q.111** If you drove from Sydney to the Blue Mountains, in which compass direction would you be travelling?

**Q.112** Which cave system is a noted feature of the Blue Mountains?

**Q.113** What is the most famous landmark in the Blue Mountains: the Twelve Apostles, the Den of Nargun, Chambers Pillar, the Three Sisters or Uluru?

**Q.114** For what beverage is the Hunter Valley noted: orange juice, wine, milk, tea or coffee?

**Q.115** The town of Tamworth is famous for an annual festival celebrating which form of music: rock, classical, country, rap or folk?

**Q.116** If you travelled the Fossickers Way across the New England Tableland, would you hope to find wildflowers, gemstones, waterfalls, fossils or birds?

**Q.117** True or false? The Warrumbungle Mountains are the remains of a volcano some 50 km wide.

**Q.118** Pick the two which are NOT Sydney beaches: Coogee, Manly, Bondi, Scarborough, Cottesloe.

**Q.119** What are Bongil Bongil, Booti Booti and Bundjalung: Aboriginal bands, national parks or brands of bushwalking footwear?

**Q.120** When was Sydney Harbour Bridge opened: 1930, 1931, 1932, 1933 or 1934?

Sydney Harbour Bridge

**Q.121** True or false? At Parkes, scientists monitor earthquakes.

**Q.122** Which two of these crops are grown in coastal northern New South Wales: sugar, wheat, bananas, apples or cherries.

**Q.123** True or false? The poor soils of northern coastal New South Wales are not suitable for forest growth.

**Q.124** What is mined at Lightning Ridge: emerald, opal, diamond, ruby or sapphire?

**Q.125** True or false? There were once huge freshwater lakes in south-western New South Wales.

**Q.126** What is the underground water reservoir which is tapped by New South Wales's inland graziers?

**Q.127** What does the expression "back of Bourke" mean: a long way from the big city or close to the big city?

**Q.128** Armidale is the main centre for which region: New England Tableland, Atherton Tableland or Barkly Tableland?

An irrigation line

**Q.129** Which Australian politician spoke in favour of Federation at Tenterfield in 1889: Gough Whitlam, Henry Parkes, W.C. Wentworth, John Howard or John Curtin?

**Q.130** Why is the ghost town of Silverton famous?

**Q.131** How do the opal miners of White Cliffs beat the summer heat?

Sculptures near Broken Hill

**Q.132** How would you describe the country around Broken Hill: fertile, arid, mountainous, coastal, alpine?

**Q.133** What makes up the Walls of China in Mungo National Park: bricks, trees, sand dunes, coral or rocks?

**Q.134** What is the name of the irrigation area watered by the Murrumbidgee River?

**Q.135** Name one metal mined at Cobar.

Silverton Hotel

**Q.136** What precious metal was discovered at Bathurst: silver, zinc, gold, platinum or titanium?

**Q.137** Which inland New South Wales town is home to the Western Plains Zoo?

**Q.138** The town of Wentworth stands where two rivers meet: what are they?

**Q.139** What is Albury's twin city?

**Q.140** Australia's largest freshwater fish lives in the Murray River. What is it called?

Zebra may be found at Western Plains Zoo

# New South Wales

**Q.141** What famous Australian was born at Bowral?

**Q.142** Kiama has a famous coastal feature. Is it a lighthouse, a reef, a jetty, a blowhole or a marina?

**Q.143** What religion is celebrated at the Nan Tien Temple, near Wollongong?

Trawler in port, Narooma

**Q.144** What does the name "Wollongong" mean, "great steel city" or "sound of the sea"?

**Q.145** Why are towns on the inland Southern Highlands cooler than coastal Wollongong?

**Q.146** What is Ulladulla: a Rugby League team song, a town, a comic strip character's exclamation of surprise or a term of abuse for a stupid person?

**Q.147** What marine mammals were once hunted from the port of Eden?

**Q.148** For what product is the town of Bega famous: cheese, chocolate, wine, coffee or caviar?

**Q.149** On a holiday to Narooma, would you take gear for skiing, mountain climbing, fishing, abseiling or hang-gliding?

**Q.150** True or false? Australia's second-highest mountain is Mt Townshend, which is 2214 m high.

**Q.151** What creatures are common at Pebbly Beach, Murramarang: Dugongs, Yabbies, Taipans, Eastern Grey Kangaroos or Bilbies?

**Q.152** True or false? Jervis Bay is not part of New South Wales.

Wollongong

**Q.153** Into which large river did the Snowy Mountains Hydro-Electric Scheme divert water from alpine rivers?

**Q.154** What is New South Wales's largest alpine national park?

Snowy River Scheme turbine

**Q.155** True or false? The Man from Snowy River was a bushranger.

**Q.156** Why does Mt Kosciuszko have a Polish name?

**Q.157** How high is Mt Kosciuszko: 1828 m, 1928 m, 2028 m, 2128 m or 2228 m?

**Q.158** How many people were killed in the Thredbo Village land-slip in 1997?

**Q.159** What do Perisher, Smiggin Holes and Mount Selwyn have in common?

**Q.160** What introduced fish do anglers aim to catch in New South Wales's alpine country in summer?

Eastern Grey Kangaroos at Pebbly Beach

**Q.161** Which nickname is applied to Victoria: the Alpine State, the Ned Kelly State, the Yarra Beauty State, the Garden State or the Melbourne Cup State?

**Q.162** What is the floral emblem of Victoria: the Common Heath, the Murray Mallee or the Cooktown Orchid?

**Q.163** Rearrange these Victorian cities in descending order of population size: Bendigo, Geelong, Melbourne, Shepparton, Ballarat.

**Q.164** Does Victoria occupy the south-west or south-east corner of the Australian continent?

**Q.165** True or false? Victoria is the smallest State of Australia.

**Q.166** What is the area of Victoria: 127 000 km$^2$, 227 600 km$^2$ or 327 600 km$^2$?

**Q.167** How many stars feature on the flag of Victoria?

**Q.168** Is the population of Victoria just under 5 million or just under 4 million?

Melbourne Cricket Ground

**Q.169** What river flows through Melbourne city?

**Q.170** On which bank of the Yarra River does Southgate stand?

**Q.171** What is the name of the statue in front of the National Gallery of Victoria: Devil, Thinker, David, Queen Victoria, Angel?

*Angel by Deborah Halpern, National Gallery of Victoria*

**Q.172** What do the initials MCG stand for?

**Q.173** True or false? Melbourne has Australia's only metropolitan tram network.

**Q.174** Is Melbourne second- or third-largest city in Australia?

**Q.175** True or false? The cottage in which Captain Bligh's parents of lived stands in Melbourne's Fitzroy Gardens.

**Q.176** The Melbourne Cup is run on the first Tuesday of which month?

**Q.177** True or false? The World Health Organisation rates Melbourne as one of the world's least polluted cities.

**Q.178** Which railway station is the hub of Melbourne's suburban rail network?

**Q.179** What covers the shopping complex at Melbourne Central: a tiled roof, a glass cone or a golden dome?

**Q.180** What football code originated in Victoria: Soccer, Rugby, Gridiron, Rugby League or Australian Rules?

Flinders Street Station, Melbourne

# Victoria

Westgate Bridge, Melbourne

**Q.181** Which major bridge carries traffic westward from Melbourne city: Westgate, Story, The Narrows, Parramatta or Brooklyn?

**Q.182** In which year was Melbourne's historic Princess Theatre opened: 1846, 1866, 1886, 1906 or 1926?

**Q.183** Is Melbourne's annual festival called Warana, Moomba, Mardi Gras, Schutzenfest or Floriade?

**Q.184** On which bay does Melbourne stand: Corio, Western Port, Shark, Port Phillip or Rum?

**Q.185** Does the Mornington Peninsula run down the eastern or the western side of Port Phillip Bay?

**Q.186** True or false? The southern tip of the Mornington Peninsula is named Cape Schanck.

**Q.187** What is The Rip?

**Q.188** True or false? The only way to reach Phillip Island is by helicopter.

Puffing Billy in the Dandenongs

**Q.189** What marine mammals can be seen on Seal Rocks, off Phillip Island?

**Q.190** Which flightless bird would you see on Phillip Island: Emu, Little Penguin, Rhea, Southern Cassowary or Ostrich?

**Q.191** What restored steam train runs through the Dandenong Ranges: Puffing Buggy, Puffing Bully, Puffing Batty, or Puffing Billy?

**Q.192** How far from Melbourne are the Dandenong Ranges: 20 km, 50 km, 80 km, 110 km or 130 km?

**Q.193** Does Healesville Sanctuary specialise in displaying native or exotic animals?

**Q.194** Which rare Australian mammal has been bred at Healesville Sanctuary?

**Q.195** True or false? Wilsons Promontory is the most southerly point of mainland Australia.

**Q.196** Is Wilsons Promontory a national park?

**Q.197** What fuel is produced in the Latrobe Valley?

**Q.198** What is the sand barrier which divides the Gippsland Lakes from Bass Strait: 80 Mile Beach, 90 Mile Beach or 100 Mile Beach?

**Q.199** Is oil produced from wells in Bass Strait?

**Q.200** What was the Nargun?

The Den of Nargun

Little Penguin

**Q.201** After which governor of the colony of New South Wales was Gippsland named?

**Q.202** Victoria's mammal emblem lives in old-growth forests of the State's central highlands. What is it?

**Q.203** True or false? Alpine National Park is small and insignificant.

**Q.204** Are Victoria's eastern mountains known as the Ski Country, the Fly Country, the High Country or the Pie in the Sky Country?

**Q.205** What is Victoria's highest peak, Mt Kosciuszko, Mt Bogong, Mt Buffalo, Mt Buller or Mt Hotham?

**Q.206** True or false? The Snow Gum is the only tree to survive above the snow line.

**Q.207** What are three recreational activities carried out in the Victoria's High Country in summer?

Leadbeater's Possum

**Q.208** Does the skiing season in the Australian Alps open in December or June?

**Q.209** What precious metal was discovered at Ballarat and Bendigo in 1850?

Replica of the Eureka Stockade, Ballarat

**Q.210** In 1854, Ballarat miners rebelled against a licensing system they thought unjust. Where did conflict take place?

**Q.211** What do the towns of Ararat, Daylesford, Castlemaine and Stawell have in common?

**Q.212** What is the modern name for the beer first brewed in Castlemaine in 1859?

**Q.213** What sporting event takes place at Stawell each year?

**Q.214** What four-man gang robbed the Jerilderie bank in 1879?

**Q.215** About how long is the Murray River: 1500 km, 2000 km, 2500 km, 3000 km or 3500 km?

**Q.216** True or false? The Murray flows to the sea at Lake Alexandrina, Victoria.

**Q.217** Give two reasons why the Murray is gradually becoming saltier.

**Q.218** What is a paddlesteamer?

**Q.219** What were paddlesteamers used for on the Murray in the 1800s?

**Q.220** True or false? The only place to see a paddlesteamer today is in a museum.

Mt Bogong

A paddlesteamer on the Murray River

Mt Arapiles

Rock formation in the Grampians

**Q.228** What name is given to central western Victoria: the Wimmera, the Woomera, the Woma, the Wobbera or the Womenera?

**Q.229** What sport is carried out at Mt Arapiles?

**Q.230** True or false? The Grampians are the western end of the Great Dividing Range.

**Q.231** Do the landowners of Victoria's Western Districts farm camels, buffalo, dairy cattle, goats, sheep or alpacas?

**Q.221** Rearrange these towns in the order you would come to them travelling east to west down the Murray River: Echuca, Swan Hill, Albury-Wodonga, Mildura, Robinvale.

**Q.222** What river is dammed at Lake Hume?

**Q.223** Does the Victoria/New South Wales border run along the northern or the southern bank of the Murray River?

**Q.224** Into which State does the Murray flow after leaving Victoria?

**Q.225** What is the name given to the dry north-western corner of Victoria: the Brigalow, the Rocks, the Mallee, the Mulga or the Pinnacles?

**Q.226** True or false? A mallee is a eucalypt tree with a tall, straight single trunk.

**Q.227** What material does the Mallee Fowl use to make its nest?

Mallee Fowl on nest

**Q.232** Is Portland a coastal or an inland town?

**Q.233** What are the towns nearest the western and the eastern ends of the Great Ocean Road?

**Q.234** What are the Twelve Apostles?

**Q.235** True or false? Between May and October, Southern Right Whales can be seen along Victoria's south-western coast.

**Q.236** What do the *Loch Ard*, the *Cataraqui* and the *Admella* have in common?

**Q.237** Do the Otway Ranges receive high or low annual rainfall?

**Q.238** True or false? Bells Beach is the scene of an annual sailing regatta.

**Q.239** What bay has the Bellarine Peninsula on its western side?

**Q.240** What major port and industrial city stands at the northern end of the Bellarine Peninsula?

The Twelve Apostles, Port Campbell National Park

**Q.241** Why was Tasmania cut off from the Australian mainland?

**Q.242** True or false? Aboriginal people colonised Tasmania after it became an island.

Hobart and the Derwent River

**Q.243** What marsupial appears on Tasmania's Coat of Arms?

**Q.244** Is this animal common today?

**Q.245** What is Tasmania's highest mountain: Mt Vesuvius, Mt McKinley, Mt Ossa, Mt Blanc or Mt Olympus?

**Q.246** What is Tasmania's floral emblem?

**Q.247** True or false? Australia's 20 deepest and 5 longest caves are all in Tasmania.

**Q.248** In the Ice Age of about 18 000 years ago, where did Tasmania's Aborigines shelter?

**Q.249** True or false? There are no descendants of Tasmania's Aboriginal peoples surviving today.

**Q.250** Tasmania's west coast holds an Australian record for the amount of sunshine in a year. Does it hold the record for the most sunshine or the least sunshine in one year?

**Q.251** How much rain may fall on parts of Tasmania's west coast each year: more than 1 m, more than 2 m, more than 3 m, more than 4 m, or more than 5 m?

**Q.252** Which Dutch navigator sighted Tasmania in 1642?

**Q.253** What did this navigator name the island?

**Q.254** What European nation besides Britain and Holland explored the seas around Tasmania?

**Q.255** What industry did the British Government try to protect by sending settlers to Tasmania in 1803?

**Q.256** True or false? Hobart is Australia's second oldest city.

**Q.257** On which river does Hobart stand?

**Q.258** Which northern Tasmanian town was established by 1806?

**Q.259** Which Tasmanian town stands on the Tamar River?

**Q.260** True or false? The convicts sent to Tasmania were well-behaved first time offenders.

Hobart city

Launceston

**Q.261** What is the mountain by which Hobart is situated: Mt Napoleon, Mt Blamey, Mt Macarthur, Mt Wellington or Mt Cosgrove?

**Q.262** What happened to Hobart's Tasman bridge, spanning the Derwent River, in 1975: did it burn down, did it explode, was it rammed by a ship or did it collapse under a festival parade?

Richmond Bridge

**Q.263** What is memorable about the stone bridge at the town of Richmond?

**Q.264** What long-lived and rare softwood tree is found in southern Tasmania.

**Q.265** Of the following national parks, which is not a Tasmanian Wilderness World Heritage Area: Southwest, Daintree, Cradle Mountain-Lake St Clair, Walls of Jerusalem, Hartz Mountains?

**Q.266** What is hydro-electricity?

**Q.267** Why did the Tasmanian Government try to dam the lower Franklin and Gordon Rivers in the early 1980s?

**Q.268** What feared prison was active on the Tasman Peninsula from 1830 and 1877?

**Q.269** How did Port Arthur's Isle of the Dead get its name?

**Q.270** What animals discouraged convicts from escaping Port Arthur by land and by sea?

**Q.271** True or false? There is no trace of the convict days remaining at Port Arthur today.

**Q.272** What is the Tessellated Pavement?

Wineglass Bay

**Q.273** Why is Wineglass Bay so-called: because of the vineyards in the area, because it is a favourite drinking spot for locals or because of its shape?

Glacier-carved landscape in the Arthur Range

**Q.274** What element has been the major force in shaping the surface of Tasmania's south-west: wind, water, ice, sunshine or bulldozers?

**Q.275** Is wine made in Tasmania?

**Q.276** True or false? The Sydney to Hobart Yacht Race is held every four years.

**Q.277** Australia's southernmost point is in Southwest National Park. What is it called?

**Q.278** True or false? Tasmania's east coast has a milder climate than its west coast.

**Q.279** Is Tasmania's east coast known as the Moon, Heavenly or Sun Coast?

**Q.280** What is a Tasmanian Devil?

Tasmanian Devil

**Q.281** Which east coast holiday resort was once the home port for sealers and whalers?

**Q.282** Freycinet National Park took its name from a navigator from which country?

**Q.283** Are The Hazards, in Freycinet National Park, tidal quicksands, a mountain range, dangerous ocean currents, or an undersea reef?

Pandani

**Q.290** How many of the following metals are mined in Tasmania: coal, copper, gold, iron, lead, tin, zinc?

**Q.291** What is mined at Queenstown?

**Q.292** What is a Pandani?

**Q.293** How deep is Lake St Clair, more than 50 m, 100 m, 150 m, 200 m or 250 m?

**Q.294** What excavated the basin in which Lake St Clair lies?

**Q.295** What is aquaculture?

**Q.296** Name a product of Tasmanian aquaculture.

**Q.297** Is paper pulp manufactured in Tasmania?

**Q.298** How were the Bass Strait Islands formed?

**Q.299** What are two islands rising from Bass Strait?

**Q.300** What delicacies are produced on King Island?

The Hazards, Freycinet National Park

**Q.284** Name two crops that are not cultivated in Tasmania: bananas, potatoes, apples, sugar cane, lavender.

**Q.285** What medical drug is made from the opium poppies cultivated in Tasmania?

**Q.286** Which port in northern Tasmania is the terminus for the Bass Strait ferry?

**Q.287** True or false? Northern Tasmania's fertile soil is weathered from volcanic rock.

**Q.288** What is The Nut, which can be found near Stanley on the north-west coast of Tasmania?

**Q.289** True or false? North-west Tasmania has more than 4000 lakes.

Lakes in western Tasmania

# South Australia

**Q.301** Is South Australia the second- or third-largest State of Australia?

**Q.302** The floral emblem of South Australia is a desert plant. What is it?

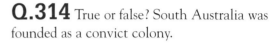

Sturt's Desert Pea

**Q.303** The "piping shrike" features on South Australia's flag and Coat of Arms. What is the modern name of this bird?

**Q.304** Which animal is the faunal emblem of South Australia: the Eastern Quoll, the Southern Hairy-nosed Wombat, the Brush-tailed Possum, the Camel or the Dingo?

**Q.305** True or false? The population of South Australia is concentrated in the north-east corner of the State?

**Q.306** True or false? 1 million of South Australia's 1 504 730 people live in the State capital city, Adelaide.

**Q.307** What is South Australia's largest lake?

**Q.308** True or false? South Australia is Australia's wettest State.

**Q.309** South-eastern South Australia has a Mediterranean climate. Are the winters warm and dry or cool and wet?

**Q.310** Is the city of Adelaide situated on the Arabian Gulf, Spencers Gulf, St Vincent Gulf, the Gulf of En or the Gulf of Guinea?

Torrens River, Adelaide

**Q.311** What are the hills to the east of Adelaide called: the Macdonnell Ranges, the Darling Ranges, the Stirling Ranges, the Mt Lofty Ranges or the Hamersley Ranges?

**Q.312** What river flows through Adelaide?

**Q.313** When was Adelaide founded: 1806, 1816, 1826, 1836 or 1846?

**Q.314** True or false? South Australia was founded as a convict colony.

**Q.315** Why is the name of Colonel William Light honoured in Adelaide?

**Q.316** How often is the Adelaide Festival of Arts held: every year, every two years, every three years, every four years?

Southern Hairy-nosed Wombat

**Q.317** What is Womadelaide: a women's festival, a world music festival or a woomera festival?

**Q.318** True or false? The Formula One Grand Prix Motor Race was for some years held in Adelaide's Rundle Mall.

**Q.319** Was Maslins Beach, south of Adelaide, the first beach in Australia: to run lifesaving carnivals, to be protected by shark netting, or on which nude bathing was allowed?

**Q.320** Which three of these crops are cultivated around Adelaide: grapes, citrus fruits, almonds, tobacco, cotton?

Grapevines in a South Australian vineyard

Historic buildings at Port Adelaide

**Q.321** What is the name of the dock area of Adelaide?

**Q.322** Is the Fleurieu Peninsula on the western or the eastern side of the St Vincent Gulf?

**Q.323** What nationality (apart from English) were many of the early settlers in the Mt Lofty Ranges?

**Q.324** What historic South Australian town is named after Dirk Hahn, captain of the ship *Zebra*?

**Q.325** What is the main product of the Barossa Valley?

**Q.326** What is South Australia's highest mountain: Mt McKinley, Mt Fuji, Mt Woodroffe, Mt Bartle Frere or Mt Eliza?

**Q.327** Why is the Murray River important to South Australia?

**Q.328** What sport is popular at Waikerie, on the River Murray: horse riding, gliding, rock-climbing, trout-fishing or surfing?

**Q.329** Through which lake does the Murray River flow to the sea: Lake Victoria, Lake Superior, Lake Eyre, Lake Alexandrina or Lake Titicaca?

The Murray River

**Q.330** What is the Coorong: a church choir, a long, narrow coastal lagoon, or an Aboriginal language?

**Q.331** Exploring caves near the town of Naracoorte, what ancient objects would you hope to find?

**Q.332** What colour is the lake near Mt Gambier in summer?

**Q.333** True or false? The most recent eruption by an Australian volcano was at Mt Gambier, 1400 years ago.

**Q.334** What adventurers would go to Ewens Ponds and Piccaninnie Ponds: cave divers, whitewater canoeists or bungee jumpers?

**Q.335** Is the eastern or the western part of the South Australian coastline called "The Crustacean Coast"?

**Q.336** Name two crustaceans.

**Q.337** To visit the Flinders Ranges, would you drive north, south, east or west of Adelaide?

**Q.338** True or false? The rocks forming the Flinders Ranges are between 1500 and 500 million years old.

**Q.339** What is Wilpena Pound, in the Flinders Ranges?

**Q.340** What world record event happened on the dry bed of Lake Eyre in the year 1964?

Wilpena Pound, Flinders Ranges

# South Australia

Cliffs on the Great Australian Bight

Opal set in a pendant

**Q.348** How many hours of sunlight per day is the average in northern South Australia: 9, 10, 11, 12, 13?

**Q.349** What is mined at Iron Knob, Iron Monarch, Iron Duke and Iron Princess?

**Q.350** True or false? Whyalla is a busy shipbuilding port.

**Q.351** What fish gave its name to Port Lincoln's Tunarama Festival?

**Q.354** What does the word Nullarbor mean?

**Q.355** What is the most common rock on the Nullarbor: granite, sandstone, basalt, limestone or dolerite?

**Q.341** True or false? Lake Eyre fills with water every second year.

**Q.342** How does water reach Lake Eyre?

**Q.343** Do Australian Pelicans breed on Lake Eyre?

**Q.344** What is mined at Andamooka and Coober Pedy?

**Q.345** How do some Coober Pedy residents avoid the heat of the Sun?

**Q.346** True or false? Much of western South Australia is under Aboriginal control.

**Q.347** Which two of the following minerals are mined at Roxby Downs: uranium, gold, silver, copper, sapphires, bauxite.

Remarkable Rocks, Kangaroo Island

**Q.352** How long is the Great Australian Bight: 700 km, 800 km, 900 km, 1000 km or 1100 km?

**Q.353** True or false? The Great Australian Bight is bordered by wide, sandy beaches.

**Q.356** Is Kangaroo Island joined to mainland South Australia?

**Q.357** What colours Remarkable Rocks red and orange?

**Q.358** What rare sea mammal breeds on Kangaroo Island at Seal Bay?

**Q.359** What rare and dangerous shark lives in the seas off South Australia?

**Q.360** What endangered giant sea mammals migrate along the coast of South Australia?

Australian Sea-lion

**Q.361** How much of mainland Australia is covered by Western Australia: one-eighth, one-quarter, one-third or one-half?

**Q.362** Of West Cape Howe and Cape Londonderry, which is Western Australia's most northerly point and which the most southerly?

**Q.363** True or false? Western Australia has only 9% of Australia's total population.

**Q.364** What is Western Australia's longest river: the Murrumbidgee, the Thames, the Roper, the Gascoyne or the Parramatta?

Perth city

**Q.365** Rank the following Western Australian cities in descending order of population: Geraldton, Boulder/Kalgoorlie, Perth, Fremantle, Albany.

**Q.366** What is the floral emblem of Western Australia?

Red and Green Kangaroo Paw

**Q.367** What is the bird emblem of Western Australia?

**Q.368** The Numbat is the mammal emblem of Western Australia. What does this rare marsupial eat?

**Q.369** Western Australia contains Australia's largest rock. What is it called: Mt Mee, Mt Augustus, Uluru or Bald Rock?

Mt Augustus

**Q.370** True or false? The Western Australian Coat of Arms bears no motto.

**Q.371** What marsupials support the shield on the Coat of Arms of Western Australia?

**Q.372** What two cities stand on the Swan River?

**Q.373** What is the capital city of Western Australia?

**Q.374** In what year did the British colonise the Swan River: 1819, 1829, 1839, or 1849?

**Q.375** True or false? British convicts were sent to Western Australia 1850–1868.

City and Scarborough Beaches

**Q.376** What do Cottesloe, Scarborough, Sorrento, City and Port have in common?

**Q.377** Why do people go to Perth's Kings Park in springtime: to play football, to water ski, to fossick for gold, to see the wildflowers or to watch Koalas?

**Q.378** How long does it take to get by fast ferry from Fremantle to Rottnest Island: 5, 10, 20, 30 or 40 minutes?

**Q.379** What are Quokkas?

**Q.380** In the south-west corner of Western Australia, does most rain fall in summer or in winter?

Admiring wildflowers in Kings Park, Perth

# Western Australia

CALM Treetop Walk, Valley of the Giants

**Q.381** The Bibbulmun Walking Track begins in Kalamunda, near Perth. Where does it end, at Kalgoorlie or at Walpole?

**Q.382** The WA Government Department which looks after National Parks is called CALM. What do these initials stand for?

**Q.383** True or false? Western Australia's native plants have developed to grow best on poor soils.

**Q.384** True or false? Perth stands on rich, dark soils with plenty of food value for plants.

**Q.385** What very tall tree is found in Western Australia's wet south-west corner: the Kurri, the Murri, the Harri, the Karri or the Sorri?

**Q.386** True or false? The Karri is the third-tallest tree in the world.

**Q.387** Name one product of Margaret River, south of Perth.

**Q.388** What family played an important part in the founding of the town of Busselton?

**Q.389** Is Bunbury inland or on the coast?

**Q.390** Which is further south, Cape Leeuwin or Cape Naturaliste?

**Q.391** Cape Leeuwin and Cape Naturaliste are named after ships. What nationalities sailed them?

**Q.392** What are the most famous features of the Valley of the Giants: big rocks, big trees, big kangaroos, big swamps or big crocodiles?

**Q.393** Name two crops which are not grown in the south-west corner of Western Australia: rice, citrus fruits, core fruits, potatoes, pineapples.

**Q.394** True or false? Torndirrup National Park, near Albany, is noted for its sandstone pillars and deep red gorges.

**Q.395** In what coastal town would you find Dog Rock, the "Amity" and Princess Royal Harbour?

The Whaling Museum and disused whale chaser, near Albany

**Q.396** What hunting industry was based near the port of Albany until 1978?

**Q.397** What are the Porongorups?

**Q.398** The Wheatbelt of Western Australia is studded with tors. Is a tor a spring, a belt of trees, a grain silo, a rocky outcrop or a stockyard?

**Q.399** What rock composes Wave Rock, near Hyden: iron ore, sandstone, granite, shale or slate?

**Q.400** What wool-producing animals are farmed in the Wheatbelt of Western Australia?

Wave Rock, near Hyden

Landmark, Kalgoorlie

**Q.410** What is Houtmans Abrolhos?

**Q.411** In 1629, which ship was wrecked on Houtmans Abrolhos: the *Duyfken*, the *Leeuwin*, the *Batavia*, the *Bounty* or the *Investigator*?

Shark Bay

**Q.401** What precious metal was discovered at Coolgardie in 1892?

**Q.402** Does Kalgoorlie/Boulder still produce gold today?

**Q.403** How is water carried to the Goldfields?

**Q.404** Is Kalgoorlie noted for its wide or its narrow streets?

**Q.405** Is Nambung National Park north or south of Perth?

**Q.406** What name is given to the limestone pillars that can be seen in Nambung National Park?

**Q.407** Around which parts of plants did these limestone pillars form?

**Q.408** What religious establishment stands at New Norcia, north of Perth: a convent, a Tibetan lamasery, a Benedictine monastery or a Buddhist temple?

**Q.409** What food delicacy is caught near Geraldton: venison, caviar, truffles, pate de foie gras or rock lobster?

The Pinnacles, Nambung National Park

**Q.412** Which river runs through Kalbarri National Park: the Moore, the Murchison, the Mitchell, the Moray or the Miranda?

**Q.413** Is Nature's Window, in Kalbarri National Park, made of wood, leaves, sand, stone or glass?

**Q.414** What were the Zuytdorp Cliffs named after: a Dutch sailing ship, a German airliner, a Liberian freighter, a French racing car or a Swiss watch?

**Q.415** What did the Dutch navigator Dirk Hartog leave on Dirk Hartog Island, Shark Bay, in 1616?

**Q.416** Is Shark Bay a World Heritage Area?

**Q.417** True or false? Shark Bay is 100 km north of Perth.

**Q.418** Which of these three crops are grown at Carnarvon: tomatoes, bananas, tobacco, beans, mushrooms.

**Q.419** Is the mid-west coast of Western Australia arid or well-watered?

**Q.420** True or false? Whales migrate up the coast of Western Australia to breed.

Nature's Window, Kalbarri National Park

# Western Australia

Bottlenose Dolphins

**Q.428** What is the port for the iron ore towns of the Hamersley region?

**Q.429** Is the town of Marble Bar renowned for being very hot in summer or very cold in winter?

**Q.430** What is the Marine Park on the seaward side of North West Cape called: Bangaloo, Wongadoo, Ningaloo, Pongaloo or Hangadoo?

**Q.431** What is the extreme northern region of Western Australia called?

Bungle Bungles, Purnululu National Park

**Q.421** What marine mammals come to shore at Monkey Mia, in Shark Bay?

**Q.422** Are Dugongs found in Shark Bay?

**Q.423** Do the stromatolites of Shark Bay represent a very ancient or a very new form of life?

**Q.424** True or false? The rocks which form the north-west of Western Australia are among the oldest known on Earth.

**Q.425** How does Mt Augustus compare in size with Uluru: the same size, twice the size or three times the size?

**Q.426** What metal is mined in the Hamersley Ranges?

**Q.427** What major national park encompasses much of the Hamersley Ranges: Kalbarri, Karakatta, Kanberra, Karijini or Katarpilla?

Boab tree

**Q.432** Does the Kimberley receive rain in the summer or in the winter?

**Q.433** What Kimberley port is noted for pearls, dinosaur footprints and camel rides along the beach?

**Q.434** True or false? The Kimberley coast is noted for its extreme tides.

**Q.435** What formed the limestone ranges of the West Kimberley: extinct volcanos, drifted sand, brown coal, ancient coral reefs or fossilised insects?

**Q.436** What is mined at Argyle in the East Kimberley?

**Q.437** Is Lake Argyle a natural or a made lake?

**Q.438** What are the Bungle Bungles?

**Q.439** True or false? The Kimberley has some of the oldest art galleries in the world.

**Q.440** What is remarkable about the trunk of the Boab tree?

Camel-riding on the beach, Broome

Sturt's Desert Rose

**Q.441** What is the floral emblem of the Northern Territory?

**Q.442** Name two seas and one gulf that border the Northern Territory.

**Q.443** True or false? The southern part of the Northern Territory is higher than the northern part.

**Q.444** What name is given to the extreme north of the Northern Territory: the Absolute End, the Top End, the High End, the Big End or the Beginning of the End?

**Q.445** Why is the south of the Northern Territory called the Red Centre?

**Q.446** What is the longest river in the Northern Territory: the Adelaide, the Elizabeth, the Victoria, the Alexandra or the Margaret?

Wedge-tailed Eagle

**Q.447** What wind system brings the Top End of the Northern Territory its rainfall: the Roaring Forties, the Monsoon, the Trade Winds, the Tsunami or the Sirocco?

**Q.448** What name is given to the Top End's summer rainy season?

**Q.449** During the "build up" to the Wet, is lightning common or uncommon?

In the Red Centre

**Q.450** What bird appears on the Coat of Arms of the Northern Territory?

**Q.451** What is the capital city of the Northern Territory?

**Q.452** True or false? Almost half of the total population of the Northern Territory live in Darwin?

**Q.453** How many air-raids did the city of Darwin survive in World War II: 44, 54, 64, 74 or 84?

**Q.454** What natural disaster hit Darwin on Christmas Day, 1974?

**Q.455** What comes to be fed at Doctors Gully, on Darwin's Esplanade: birds, kangaroos, crocodiles, goannas or fish?

**Q.456** What large reptile may sometimes be sighted in Darwin Harbour?

**Q.457** What would you expect to see at Darwin's Mindil Beach: spectacular sunsets, weekly markets or an annual Beer Can Regatta (or all three)?

**Q.458** Why is summertime swimming from Darwin's beaches not a good idea?

**Q.459** Why do people go to Fogg Dam, 60 km from Darwin: to swim, to sail, to scuba dive, to hunt kangaroos or to watch birds?

**Q.460** Where is a Frilled Lizard's (common across the Top End) frill?

Beer Can Regatta, Mindil Beach

# Northern Territory

Saltwater Crocodile, Adelaide River

**Q.461** On the Adelaide River, near Darwin, what do Saltwater Crocodiles do to obtain food: leap from the water, swim through hoops or swim upside down?

**Q.462** Is Kakadu National Park east or west of Darwin?

**Q.463** Which Aboriginal group manages Kakadu: the Noongah, the Pitjatjantjara, the Gagudju or the Yolgnu?

**Q.464** True or false? There is no Aboriginal rock art in Kakadu National Park.

**Q.465** How long have Aboriginal people been present in the Top End: at least 20 000, 30 000 or 40 000 years?

**Q.466** The Arnhem Land Escarpment runs through Kakadu. What is an escarpment?

**Q.467** Which two birds of the following would not be seen in Kakadu: albatross, gannet, egret, cormorant, ibis?

**Q.468** What has made some people concerned for Kakadu's World Heritage status: cattle grazing, mining, motor racing, crocodile hunting or venomous snakes?

**Q.469** What is mined at Jabiru: gold, opals, uranium, diamonds or bauxite?

**Q.470** A large motel in the town of Jabiru is an unusual shape. What does it resemble?

Aboriginal rock art, Kakadu National Park

**Q.471** What are termites?

**Q.472** Why are magnetic termite mounds so-called: because they draw iron objects to them; because they are oriented north-south or because they are shaped like horseshoe magnets?

**Q.473** Is Borroloola in the north-east or the south-east of the Northern Territory?

**Q.474** What is Groote Eylandt?

**Q.475** What is Victoria River Downs: a cattle station, a bed and breakfast establishment, a waterfall, a racecourse or a brand of beer?

**Q.476** Do Boab trees grow in the north-west of the Northern Territory?

**Q.477** What is the major highway that runs southwards from Darwin called: the Eyre, Sturt, Stuart, Oxley or Hume Highway?

**Q.478** What river has carved out the gorges of Nitmiluk National Park: the Mary, the Ellen, the Victoria, the Annie or the Katherine?

**Q.479** What town stands on the Katherine River?

**Q.480** What is Mataranka noted for: caves, waterfalls, thermal springs, blowholes or meteor craters?

Magnetic Termite mounds, Litchfield National Park

**Q.481** What book was set at Elsey Station, on the Roper River, *We of the Never-Never* or *Robbery Under Arms?*

**Q.482** How far is it from Darwin to Alice Springs: 1208 km, 1308 km, 1408 km, 1508 km or 1608 km?

**Q.483** True or false? The Stuart Highway is noted for its hairpin bends and steep zig-zags.

**Q.484** What are the Devil's Marbles?

**Q.485** What extensive grassland lies to the east of the Stuart Highway: the Darling Downs, the Barkly Tableland or the Gippsland Plains?

**Q.486** What was the original name of Alice Springs: Sturt, Stuart, Lasseter, Leichhardt or Kennedy?

**Q.487** On which river does Alice Springs stand: the Torrens, the Henley, the Finke, the Todd or the Alice?

Chambers Pillar

**Q.488** What is remarkable about the boats used in the annual Alice Springs sailing regatta?

**Q.489** True or false? Alice Springs was the site of an Overland Telegraph repeater station built in the 1870s.

The Ochre Pits, MacDonnell Ranges

**Q.490** What lifesaving service was begun by Dr John Flynn?

**Q.491** What are the ranges which extend across Central Australia for 400 km?

**Q.492** Is Chambers Pillar south or north of Alice Springs?

**Q.493** What does Chambers Pillar represent in traditional Aboriginal belief?

**Q.494** What semiprecious stones were found at Ruby Gap, in the East MacDonnell Ranges?

**Q.495** What is the name of the trail that runs along the crest of the West MacDonnell Ranges: the Allamanda Trail, the Jacaranda Trail, the Portulacca Trail or the Larapinta Trail?

**Q.496** What pigment used by Aborigines to decorate their bodies was mined in the MacDonnell Ranges?

**Q.497** True or false? The rivers in the MacDonnell Ranges run deep and strong.

**Q.498** Which gap in the MacDonnells is only 22 km west of Alice Springs: Jessie Gap, Emily Gap, Trephina Gorge, Simpsons Gap or N'Dharla Gorge?

**Q.499** What colour is the trunk of a Ghost Gum?

**Q.500** What rainforest trees grow in Central Australia's Palm Valley?

The Devil's Marbles

Ghost Gum

Kata Tjuṯa

**Q.510** How high does Uluru rise above the desert: nearly 250 m, nearly 300 m, nearly 350 m or nearly 400 m?

**Q.511** Is Kata Tjuṯa one rounded rock or a number of domes?

**Q.512** Is the summit of Mt Olga higher or lower than that of Uluru?

Dingo

**Q.501** Which natural feature is the centrepiece of Watarrka National Park: Queens Pool, Twin Falls, Mungo Lake, Dingo Swamp or Kings Canyon?

**Q.502** True or false? Rainbow Valley is so-called because of the brilliant colours of the fish caught in its claypans after rain.

**Q.503** How far south-west of Alice Springs is Uluru-Kata Tjuṯa National Park: 370 km, 470 km, 570 km, 670 km or 770 km?

**Q.504** True or false? Aeroplanes are not allowed to land near Uluru.

**Q.505** Is Uluru the biggest rock in Australia?

**Q.506** True or false? Two-third of Uluru lies beneath the ground.

**Q.507** What is the town near Uluru where visitors stay: Yulara, Alice Springs, Katherine, Xanadu or Kata Tjuṯa?

**Q.508** Who are Anangu?

**Q.509** Do Anangu approve of people climbing Uluru?

Uluru and wildflowers

**Q.513** Of what rock are Uluru and Kata Tjuṯa composed: limestone, granite, basalt, sandstone or pumice?

**Q.514** Which three States share borders with the Northern Territory?

**Q.515** True or false? In some places in the Red Centre it may not rain for several years.

**Q.516** Are wildflowers ever seen in Central Australia?

**Q.517** In which corner of the Northern Territory is the Simpson Desert?

**Q.518** What desert is found in the central west of the Northern Territory: the Tanami, the Warrabi, the Womblebi, the Nevertri or the Narrabri?

**Q.519** What wild dog lives in Central Australia?

**Q.520** True or false? Central Australia once had mountains which were higher than the Himalayas are today.

Driving around Uluru

# Queensland

Cooktown Orchid

The Brisbane River

**Q.529** What is Queensland's bird emblem?

**Q.530** What is the meaning of Queensland's motto, *Audax at Fidelis*?

**Q.531** List these cities in descending order of population size: Cairns, Mount Isa, Townsville, Brisbane, Gold Coast/Tweed.

**Q.521** What percentage of the area of Australia is taken up by Queensland?

**Q.522** What is Queensland's floral emblem?

**Q.523** True or false? About one-quarter of Australian Aborigines live in Queensland.

**Q.524** Is the population of Queensland nearest 1.5, 2.5, 3.5 or 4.5 million?

**Q.525** How many corners has south-western Queensland?

**Q.526** What is the name of the corner where Queensland meets New South Wales and South Australia?

**Q.527** True or false? A Red Deer supports one side of the shield on Queensland's Coat of Arms.

**Q.528** What is Queensland's mammal emblem?

South Bank Beach, South Bank Parklands and the Brisbane River

**Q.532** Queensland has the wettest town in Australia. Is it Weipa, Roma, Toowoomba, Tully or Kanungra?

**Q.533** Which major Queensland city stands on Moreton Bay?

**Q.534** True or false? The original Aboriginal inhabitants of Moreton Bay hunted fish with the help of wild dolphins.

**Q.535** On which river does Brisbane stand?

**Q.536** True or false? The Brisbane River is tidal and salt water may reach up to 90 km upstream.

**Q.537** Is South Bank Parklands on the north or the south bank of the Brisbane River?

**Q.538** When does Brisbane receive the major part of its rainfall, April–September or October–March?

**Q.539** True or false? Brisbane was settled as a prison for the worst convicts from New South Wales.

**Q.540** Brisbane has two botanic gardens, one in the city. Where is the other: at Mt Nebo, Mt Glorious, Mt Coot-tha, Mt Mee or Mt Coonowrin?

Mt Coot-tha Botanic Gardens

Koala

Subtropical rainforest, Lamington National Park

**Q.541** How long would it take to drive (at legal speeds) from Brisbane to the Gold Coast: 30 minutes, 60 minutes, 90 minutes or 120 minutes?

**Q.542** The Gold Coast stretches south from the mouth of the Coomera River to the mouth of which river: the Bremer, the Pine, the Tweed or the Noosa?

**Q.543** Which nectar-eating parrot comes in flocks to Currumbin Sanctuary to be fed?

**Q.544** What marine mammals would you expect to see at Sea World on the Gold Coast?

**Q.545** What do Dreamworld, Movie World, the Indy Carnival and the Magic Millions have in common?

**Q.546** True or false? The Gold Coast is so-called because gold was mined there.

**Q.547** Are the McPherson Ranges part of the Great Dividing Range?

**Q.548** On the border of which two States are the McPherson Ranges?

**Q.549** What type of rainforest exists in Lamington National Park: cool temperate, subtropical or tropical?

**Q.550** What two things would you not see in Lamington National Park: sand dunes, strangler figs, freshwater crayfish, waterfalls, sandstone domes?

The Gold Coast

**Q.551** True or false? South-eastern Queensland has never been a volcanic area.

**Q.552** What major highway runs north from Brisbane: the Warrego, the Hume, the Bruce, the Stuart or the Eyre?

**Q.553** What are the volcanic peaks just north of Brisbane called?

**Q.554** True or false? The Sunshine Coast is south of Brisbane.

**Q.555** What do Maroochydore, Noosa, Mooloolaba and Caloundra have in common?

**Q.556** Are Mapleton, Maleny and Montville coastal or inland towns?

**Q.557** Which three crops are grown in the Sunshine Coast hinterland: pineapples, sugar cane, cherries, wheat, avocados?

**Q.558** Why is Fraser Island remarkable?

**Q.559** How high can Fraser Island's sand dunes rise: 50 m, 100 m, 150 m, 200 m or 250 m?

**Q.560** Is Fraser Island World Heritage listed?

The Glass House Mountains

**Q.561** Hervey Bay is the base for a fleet of tourist-carrying vessels. What are the tourists doing?

**Q.562** What species of whale migrates up the eastern Australian coast to breed?

**Q.563** Lady Elliot Island is at the southern end of the Great Barrier Reef. What island is at the northern end?

Moored craft,
Whitsunday Islands

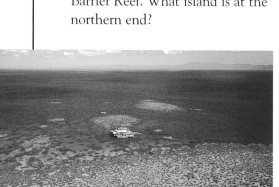

The Great Barrier Reef, a World Heritage Area

**Q.564** True or false? The Great Barrier Reef is made up of around 2500 small reefs.

**Q.565** Can the Great Barrier Reef be seen from space?

**Q.566** True or false? There have been coral reefs on Queensland's northern coast for up to 18 million years.

**Q.567** What year was the Great Barrier Reef declared a World Heritage area: 1951, 1961, 1971, 1981 or 1991?

**Q.568** How could global warming affect the Great Barrier Reef?

**Q.569** What do Dunk, Lizard, Hayman, Green and Heron Islands have in common?

**Q.570** What ore is processed into aluminium in Gladstone: bauxite, ilmenite, diorite, quartzite or dolerite?

**Q.571** What Queensland town stands on the Tropic of Capricorn?

**Q.572** What meat is the Rockhampton area famous for: pork, beef, mutton, chicken or venison?

**Q.573** True or false? There are 74 islands in the Whitsunday Group.

**Q.574** What is bareboating: sailing a boat while naked, hiring a boat to sail, sinking a boat, cleaning a boat or building a boat?

**Q.575** True or false? Townsville is Queensland's sixth-largest city.

**Q.576** What is the hill which overlooks Townsville: Mansion Hill, Fort Hill, Palace Hill, Castle Hill or Humblehome Hill?

**Q.577** What island lies 8 km offshore from Townsville?

**Q.578** What is the nearest mainland town to Hinchinbrook Island: Townsville, Cardwell, Innisfail, Cairns or Port Douglas?

**Q.579** True or false? None of Hinchinbrook Island is protected as a national park.

**Q.580** What sport is popular on the Tully River?

Whitehaven Beach, Whitsunday Island

Whitewater rafting, Tully River

# Queensland

Cairns and Trinity Inlet

In the Carnarvon Ranges

**Q.581** On what inlet is Cairns situated: Gemini Inlet, Trinity Inlet, Biennial Inlet, Quatro Inlet or Cinco Inlet?

**Q.582** True or false? It is not possible to visit the Great Barrier Reef from Cairns.

**Q.583** Skyrail gondolas have a terminus at Caravonica Lakes, near Cairns. Where is their other terminus: Maleny, Babinda, Mareeba, Kuranda or Malanda?

**Q.584** What sort of forest does Skyrail pass over?

**Q.585** What is the tableland just inland from Cairns called: the Albany, Alcheringa, Alcatraz, Alhambra or Atherton Tableland?

**Q.586** Name one thing not produced on the Atherton Tableland: Macadamia nuts, tobacco, dairy cattle, oats, coffee.

**Q.587** True or false? A number of feature films have been shot at Port Douglas.

**Q.588** Does Queensland's Wet Tropics World Heritage Area only include rainforest areas from Cairns to Cooktown?

**Q.589** Which navigator named Cape Tribulation?

**Q.590** Approximately how far is the tip of Cape York Peninsula from Cairns along the most direct route: 650 km, 750 km, 850 km, 950 km or 1050 km?

**Q.591** Name an island off the tip of Cape York Peninsula.

**Q.592** Does the Warrego Highway run northwards, westwards or southwards from Brisbane?

**Q.593** What is the rich farming area whose major centre is Toowoomba?

**Q.594** What is the Granite Belt: a line of hills, a wine- and fruit-growing area, a rugby team or an alcoholic drink?

**Q.595** True or false? The Carnarvon Ranges are outliers of the Great Dividing Range.

**Q.596** Where does water for central Queensland's sheep and cattle industries come from?

**Q.597** Where is the Channel Country, in Queensland's south-west or north-west?

**Q.598** What is the normal population of Birdsville: around 50, around 100, around 150, around 200 or around 250?

Birdsville Hotel, Birdsville

**Q.599** Which ores are mined at Mt Isa: gold, copper, silver, lead, zinc?

**Q.600** Why is Riversleigh, in Queensland's north-west, famous amongst palaeontologists?

Skyrail gondola above the rainforest

Duntroon, Canberra

**Q.601** True or false? Canberra was created to be Australia's National Capital.

**Q.602** True or false? There was no European settlement on the site of Canberra until 1913.

**Q.603** What was the name of the property Sydney merchant Robert Campbell took up in 1825: Puckoon, Muldoon, Tantroon, Duntroon or Krazytoon?

**Q.604** The oldest building in the ACT is Blundell's Farmhouse. Was it built in 1860 or in 1880?

**Q.605** When was the site for the ACT acquired by the Commonwealth Government: 1907, 1908, 1909, 1910 or 1911?

**Q.606** Why is the Australian Capital Territory sited where it is?

**Q.607** While the site for Canberra was decided, where did Australia's Federal Parliament sit: Sydney, Melbourne, Brisbane, Perth or Adelaide?

**Q.608** True or false? The Australian Capital Territory occupies 10% of the area of Australia.

Blundell's Farmhouse, Canberra

**Q.609** What is the longest river that flows through the Australian Capital Territory?

**Q.610** What is the highest point of the Australian Capital Territory?

**Q.611** What bay gives the Australian Capital Territory a sea port: Botany Bay, Bingle Bay, Jervis Bay, Pearl Bay or Moreton Bay?

**Q.612** How long is the coastline of the ACT: 15 km, 35 km, 55 km, 75 km or 95 km?

**Q.613** What does the word Canberra mean: a shouting place, a fighting place, a sleeping place, a hunting place or a meeting place?

**Q.614** Who planned Canberra?

**Q.615** True or false? Walter Burley Griffin was an Australian town planner.

**Q.616** When did Walter Burley Griffin finally leave Canberra: 1917, 1918, 1919, 1920 or 1921?

**Q.617** What river was impeded to make Lake Burley Griffin: the Murray, the Molonglo, the Darling, the Cooper or the Hawkesbury?

**Q.618** In what year was Lake Burley Griffin flooded: 1944, 1954, 1964, 1974 or 1984?

**Q.619** What is the ACT's faunal emblem?

**Q.620** True or false? Nearly half of the ACT is set aside for parks and reserves.

Gang-Gang Cockatoo

Lake Burley Griffin, Canberra

# Australian Capital Territory

Parliament House on Capital Hill, Canberra

**Q.621** What is the floral emblem of the Australian Capital Territory?

**Q.622** What is the difference between the two swans which support the shield on the Territory's Coat of Arms?

**Q.623** Does the flag of the ACT feature the Southern Cross?

**Q.624** True or false? Canberra's coldest recorded ground temperature is -15.1°C.

**Q.625** True or false? From 1913 to 1928 the sale of alcohol was not allowed in the Australian Capital Territory.

**Q.626** When was self government granted to the Australian Capital Territory: 1959, 1969, 1979, 1989 or 1999?

**Q.627** Which parliament sits in Canberra?

**Q.628** What two bodies make up Australia's Federal Parliament?

**Q.629** When did Federal Parliament move to Canberra?

Captain Cook Memorial Water Jet

**Q.630** When was the present Parliament House completed?

**Q.631** On which hill is Parliament House sited?

**Q.632** True or false? Much of Parliament House is sunk in the ground.

**Q.633** Can the public walk across the roof of Parliament House?

**Q.634** How many rooms are there in Parliament House: 2500, 3000, 3500, 4000 or 4500?

**Q.635** True or false? The mosaic in the forecourt of Parliament House copies an old Italian design.

**Q.636** How many days a year is Parliament House closed to the public?

**Q.637** How long is the shoreline of Lake Burley Griffin: 36 km, 37 km, 38 km, 39 km or 40 km?

**Q.638** What explorer's name is given to the water jet in Lake Burley Griffin?

**Q.639** How high does the water jet in Lake Burley Griffin rise: 107 m, 117 m, 127 m, 137 m or 147 m?

**Q.640** About what percentage of Canberra's residents work for the government: 10%, 20%, 30%, 40% or 50%?

Balloons rising from the shore of Lake Burley Griffin

Mosaic forecourt, Parliament House, Canberra

The Telstra Tower, Canberra

**Q.641** On what mountain does the Telstra Tower stand: White Mountain, Red Mountain, Green Mountain, Black Mountain or Blue Mountain?

**Q.642** How high is the Telstra Tower: 155.2 m, 165.2 m, 175.2 m, 185.2 m or 195.2 m?

**Q.643** What do the initials AIS stand for?

**Q.644** When was the AIS founded: 1979, 1980, 1981, 1982 or 1983?

**Q.645** Can the public use facilities such as pools and courts at the AIS?

**Q.646** What is displayed at the National Gallery of Australia?

The National Gallery of Australia, Canberra

**Q.647** What is the popular name for the National Science and Technology Centre?

**Q.648** This centre (Q.647) was built in 1988 as a joint project with which country: Japan, India, Korea, Indonesia or Vietnam?

**Q.649** If you went to Duntroon College in Canberra, what profession would you have entered?

Springtime brings Floriade to Canberra

**Q.650** What avenue leads to the Australian War Memorial: Dunkirk Avenue, Alamein Avenue, Anzac Avenue, Ypres Avenue or Kokoda Avenue?

**Q.651** Who lies in the grave in the Hall of Memory of the Australian War Memorial?

**Q.652** Beside Lake Burley Griffin is a monument shaped as a terrestrial globe. Which British navigator does it commemorate?

**Q.653** What lake lies beside Commonwealth Park?

The National Science and Technology Centre

**Q.654** In September-October of each year, what festival of flowers is held in Canberra: Floribunda, Floriade, Florafest, Floramagnifica or Florapolisha?

**Q.655** True or false? The leaves of Canberra's deciduous trees stay the same colour all the year round.

**Q.656** What is displayed at the Australian National Botanic Garden?

**Q.657** True or false? Canberra is Australia's foggiest city.

**Q.658** True or false? Some suggestions for names for the National Capital included Meladneyperbane, Cooeeton and Kangermu.

**Q.659** Tidbinbilla is 40 km from Canberra. What link has it with the United States of America?

**Q.660** What national park covers about 40% of the Australian Capital Territory: Nudgee, Narrabri, Namatjira, Namadgi or Naturaliste?

**Q.661** How thick is the crust of the Earth: up to 50 km, up to 100 km, up to 150 km or up to 200 km?

**Q.662** Is the crust thinner or thicker under the continents?

**Q.663** What is magma?

**Q.664** True or false? Australia floats on a soft ocean of molten rock.

**Q.665** Do the continents still drift around the Earth?

**Q.666** How long ago were the most ancient rocks on Australia's surface formed: 5000, 4300 or 3600 million years b.p. (before the present)?

**Q.667** Until around 55 million years ago, Australia was joined to a huge land mass. What do we call this land mass: Siluria, Dinosauria, Gondwana, Utopia or Antipodia?

**Q.668** What was the final continent from which Australia separated: Africa, America, Asia or Antarctica?

**Q.669** Is Australia still moving northwards?

Mountains formed by layers of sandstone being squeezed and pushed upwards

**Q.670** What are formed when continental masses come together and the Earth's crust is pushed upwards?

**Q.671** What forms deep ocean trenches: downwards buckling of the Earth's crust, digging by deep sea animals or gouging by rocks carried by ocean currents?

**Q.672** True or false? Sedimentary rocks are formed from layers of mud, sand or silt deposited by water.

Volcanic plug formed of cooled lava

**Q.673** How are igneous rocks formed: from layers of sand deposited by wind and water, by the cooling of magma forced to the Earth's surface or from the remains of coral reefs?

**Q.674** True or false? Fine-grained igneous rocks cooled rapidly, coarser-grained ones cooled more slowly.

Jasper is a metamorphic rock, changed by heat and pressure.

**Q.675** What are the igneous rocks in this group: granite, jasper, limestone, basalt, pumice?

**Q.676** What is lava?

**Q.677** What forms a volcano?

**Q.678** What is a fossil?

**Q.679** In which four of the following places have fossils been found: Naracoorte (SA), Riversleigh (Q), caves on the Nullarbor Plain (WA, SA), Mt Kosciuszko (NSW), Dinosaur Cove (V)?

**Q.680** What evidence is there that Australia was once joined to South Africa, South America and Antarctica?

Fossil of fern leaves

Rainwater eroding rock by softening and dissolving it.

**Q.681** What is the six-letter word beginning with "s" used for layers of rock?

**Q.682** A metamorphic rock has been "cooked". What was responsible for the cooking?

**Q.683** True or false? Slate, gneiss and quartzite are all metamorphic rocks.

**Q.684** What are three forces which erode the exposed surface of the Earth?

**Q.685** How does a sudden change in temperature break up rock?

**Q.686** True or false? Windblown sand has little effect on rock.

**Q.687** How do plants help break up rock?

**Q.688** True or false? Rainwater contains chemicals which wear away rock.

**Q.689** Does pollution with industrial chemicals slow or hasten the process of chemical weathering of rock?

**Q.690** True or false? About 97% of the world's water is in the oceans.

A plunge pool forms at the foot of a waterfall.

**Q.691** What is a glacier?

**Q.692** True or false? There have never been any glaciers in Australia.

**Q.693** Were Tasmania's cirque lakes carved out by water, by wind, by sand or by ice?

Water wears away rock.

Plant roots break up rock by pressure and chemical action.

**Q.694** Does a glacier carve out a V-shaped or a U-shaped valley?

**Q.695** When a bend or loop of a river becomes cut off, by what Aboriginal name is it known in Australia?

**Q.696** What is the term for the fan-shaped area where a river broadens or breaks up to enter the sea: an alpha, a beta, a gamma, a delta or an epsilon?

**Q.697** When does moving water drop the sediment it carries: when its flow becomes faster or when it slows down?

**Q.698** Where would you find a plunge pool: at the base of coastal cliffs, at the foot of a waterfall or in an ocean current?

**Q.699** True or false? Winter snow covers only about 0.3% of Australia's land surface.

**Q.700** Are the Australian Alps in south-eastern or south-western Australia?

The Warrumbungles are remnants of ancient volcanoes.

**Q.701** Above what height does winter snow fall in Australia: 1100 m, 1200 m, 1300 m, 1400 m?

**Q.702** Where do Australia's snow-bearing winds come from: Africa, Europe, South America or Antarctica?

**Q.703** Are there any active volcanos in Australia today?

**Q.704** Australia's most recent volcanic eruption was in western Victoria. Was it 13 million or 13 thousand years ago?

**Q.705** What mountain is the remnants of the central plug of the extinct Tweed Volcano, in north-eastern New South Wales?

**Q.706** How were the Warrumbungles, NSW, formed: from sedimentary rocks pushed up by earth movements or by volcanic eruptions?

**Q.707** True or false? Lord Howe Island is the remains of a huge undersea volcano.

**Q.708** What do the Organ Pipes (V), Fingal Head (NSW), the Undara Lava Tubes (Q) and Cradle Mountain (T) have in common?

**Q.709** How are the basalt and dolerite that come from old volcanic necks used: as "blue metal" in road construction, in beauty aids, for building rock gardens or as good luck charms?

**Q.710** What do Wave Rock (WA), Remarkable Rocks (SA) and Bald Rock (NSW) have in common?

**Q.711** True or false? Precious stones are never found on the sites of old volcanos.

**Q.712** Is Nature's Window, in Kalbarri National Park, WA, made of igneous, sedimentary or metamorphic rock?

**Q.713** What rock forms the Arnhem Land Escarpment, NT: limestone, shale, granite, sandstone or basalt?

**Q.714** True or false? Uluru and Kata Tjuta are too massive ever to be worn away by erosion.

**Q.715** At Wilpena in the Flinders Ranges, SA, rock has been bent to form a vast saucer. Is this called a paddock, a pound, a room, a basin or a yard?

**Q.716** When rock strata break and slip, what are the breaks called: accidents, problems, faults, blames or disasters?

A mountain range formed by a giant anticline

**Q.717** Is an upward fold in rock strata called a syncline or an anticline?

**Q.718** What substance may eventually form petroleum gas and oil?

**Q.719** Is coal of animal, mineral or vegetable origin?

**Q.720** Name two coastal areas where petroleum or gas is mined in Australia.

The Organ Pipes, V, were formed as hot lava cooled and cracked to form columns.

**Q.721** True or false? Tasmania's Federation Peak is composed of metamorphic quartzite and schist.

**Q.722** What metamorphic rock forms the red and white "marble" at Marble Bar, WA: quartzite, schist, slate, jasper or gneiss?

**Q.723** What is the common name for solid-form silica: mud, dust, boulders, sand or stones?

**Q.724** What is a duricrust: a hard layer of rock which caps softer rocks or a part of a river bed resistant to erosion?

**Q.725** What four of the following landforms have flat tops: mesa, butte, spire, tableland, plateau.

**Q.726** What is a gibber plain?

**Q.727** Does water sink through limestone fast or slowly?

**Q.728** Stalactites and stalagmites are formed by dropping water depositing minerals. Which go up and which go down?

Federation Peak, T, is made of eroded metamorphic rocks.

**Q.729** What is the large cave complex in the Blue Mountains?

This dune is made of silica.

**Q.730** True or false? There are many caves under the Nullarbor Plain.

**Q.731** True or false? No animals live in caves.

**Q.732** What carries salt into Lake Eyre?

**Q.733** The Napier Range, in the Kimberley of WA, is made of limestone. How can we deduce that this area was once under the sea?

**Q.734** True or false? The artesian water used at Yulara (Ulu<u>r</u>u) Resort, NT, is estimated to be 7000 years old.

**Q.735** Are Australia's wetlands safe from chemical pollution?

**Q.736** What is the name given to water sweeping up or down a beach from breaking waves: swish, swash, swoosh, swuz or swesh?

**Q.737** What do the sites of Brisbane, Sydney, Melbourne, Adelaide, Hobart and Perth have in common?

**Q.738** Is Sydney Harbour a drowned river valley?

**Q.739** Along the coast of the Kimberley, WA, what is the greatest difference between low and high tide: 6 m, 8 m, 10 m, 12 m or 14 m?

**Q.740** What formed the Twelve Apostles on the Victorian south-west coast?

Gibbers are rounded pebbles weathered from a hard crust of rock.

The cliffs of Geikie Gorge, WA, were once a succession of coral reefs.

Size determines whether this is a shrub or a tree.

As old bark peels off, new bark takes its place.

**Q.741** Which two of the following are not plants: fungi, ferns, lichens, pine trees, banksias.

**Q.742** Are mushrooms plants or fungi?

**Q.743** True or false? Plants can make their own food substances.

**Q.744** What is needed for green plants to make food: heat, cold, darkness, sunshine or vacuum?

**Q.745** Is water necessary or unnecessary for plant growth?

**Q.746** What colour is chlorophyll: red, yellow, blue, green or black?

**Q.747** True or false? Chlorophyll harnesses the power of sunlight to produce food substances in the green parts of plants.

**Q.748** Can a plant consist of a single cell?

**Q.749** What is the wall of a plant cell made of: skin, cellulose, protein, rock or varnish?

**Q.750** True or false? The cell walls of plants are rigid and cannot expand or bend.

**Q.751** What watery substance is present in plant tissue: blood, lymph, sludge, sap or tears?

Lichen

**Q.752** What is the fibrous tissue in the trunk of a tree called?

**Q.753** Do herbaceous plants have woody stems or soft stems?

**Q.754** Do plant stems and leaves grow towards light or towards darkness?

**Q.755** Can any plants survive in complete darkness?

**Q.756** What is the outer covering of the stem or trunk of a plant called?

**Q.757** What is one function of plant roots?

**Q.758** What is the difference between a shrub and a tree?

**Q.759** Do plants grow on desert sand dunes?

**Q.760** What is the name given to a plant growing in the wrong place: a weed, a cutting, a seed, a sprout or a graft?

Roots help hold a plant in place.

**Q.761** True or false? Algae are plants.

**Q.762** What algae are commonly seen having drifted on to a beach or growing in seawater?

**Q.763** Is the Giant Kelp of Australia's southern coasts an alga?

**Q.764** How does Giant Kelp keep its long strands afloat?

**Q.765** What algae are dangerous to life in inland waterways?

**Q.766** True or false? Seaweeds may be brown, green or red.

**Q.767** What are microscopic algae floating in the sea in great numbers called: wrack, plankton, drift, jetsam, flotsam?

**Q.768** True or false? Ferns developed only in the past few million years.

Seaweed is a form of alga.

**Q.769** Would you look for ferns in dry or in damp habitats?

**Q.770** Do ferns reproduce by seeds or by spores?

Ferns grow well along watercourses and in gullies.

**Q.771** What is the common name for a conifer: a beech tree, an oak tree, a pine tree, an aspen tree or an elm tree?

**Q.772** True or false? Conifers have thin, needle-like or scale-like leaves.

**Q.773** What do the names Wollemi, Bunya, Hoop, Norfolk Island and Cypress have in common?

**Q.774** Where was the ancient Wollemi Pine recently discovered: the Daintree River, the Great Ocean Road, the Nullarbor Plain, the Blue Mountains or the Grampians?

**Q.775** Are flowering plants the oldest or most recent form of plants?

**Q.776** What is a flower's function: digestive, defensive, reproductive or offensive?

**Q.777** True or false? Many Australian plants have flowers which produce sweet nectar.

**Q.778** Why are animals attracted to nectar-producing flowers?

**Q.779** True or false? Moths, birds and mammals carry pollen from the male parts to the female parts of a flower.

**Q.780** After pollen fertilises a flower's female parts, what is produced: a leaf, a bud, a root, a stem or a seed?

Flowering plants developed comparatively recently.

Bunya Pine

# Australia's Plants

This Scaly-breasted Lorikeet pollinates flowers as it eats nectar.

**Q.781** What are two ways in which a flower draws an animal's attention to itself?

**Q.782** Which of the following animals pollinate plants: flying-fox (fruit-bat), wallaby, butterfly, Honey-possum, bee?

**Q.783** True or false? Male wasps may try to mate with orchid flowers which resemble female wasps.

**Q.784** How is the pollen of grasses dispersed: on the tails of animals, on the wind, by water, by gravity or by humans?

**Q.785** Are some people allergic to pollen?

**Q.786** What is the fleshy protection for a seed or seeds called?

**Q.787** What is the popular name for eucalyptus fruits?

Eucalyptus fruits, also known as gumnuts

**Q.788** Where is it best for a seed to grow into a healthy plant: under the parent plant or far from the parent plant?

**Q.789** What are two ways for seeds to spread away from the parent plant?

**Q.790** An Australian eucalypt is the tallest flowering plant in the world. What is it?

**Q.791** The record for a Mountain Ash, for a tree felled in 1872 in Victoria, was how many metres: 90, 110, 130, 150 or 170?

Sundews are insectivorous plants.

**Q.792** How old was the oldest Huon pine felled in Tasmania, 1500 or 2500 years?

**Q.793** What are two sorts of Australian plants that trap and digest insects?

Mountain Ash

**Q.794** Which Australian trees are widely grown overseas, where they are used for fuel, oil and shade?

**Q.795** What swollen-trunked tree appears in both Australia and Africa?

**Q.796** True or false? Before Europeans arrived, nearly all of Australia was covered by forests.

**Q.797** Who gave his name to the banksias?

**Q.798** Which explorer had a desert pea flower and a desert hibiscus named after him?

**Q.799** True or false? The wildflower industry is worth millions of dollars to Australia.

**Q.800** Why do possums and gliders disappear when old growth forests are logged?

Scarlet Banksia

43

**Q.801** What is the difference between an invertebrate and a vertebrate animal?

**Q.802** True or false? Vertebrates make up only 5% of the world's animals.

**Q.803** Are earthworms, beetles, scorpions and spiders invertebrates or vertebrates?

**Q.804** Is the skeleton of an arthropod inside or outside its body.

Butterflies are invertebrates.

The Lamington Freshwater Cray is an arthropod.

**Q.805** Which three of the following are arthropods: housefly, crab, snail, leech, centipede.

**Q.806** How many pairs of legs has an insect: 2, 3, 4, 5 or 6?

**Q.807** True or false? Insects make up around 80% of all known animals.

A beetle is an insect.

**Q.808** True or false? The oldest insect fossils known to science come from the Carboniferous period, around 300 million years ago.

**Q.809** List three insects which can cause disease in humans.

**Q.810** What moth did the Aborigines of south-eastern Australia feast on: the Hercules Moth, the Bogong Moth, the Emperor Gum Moth, the Tiger Moth or the Zodiac Moth?

**Q.811** How many pairs of walking legs has a spider?

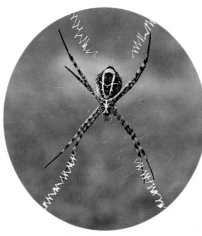

A spider in its web.

**Q.812** True or false? A spider feeds by injecting digestive juices which break down the victim's tissues, then sucking up the liquid.

**Q.813** True or false? A spider breathes through gills.

**Q.814** Does spider silk dissolve in water?

**Q.815** Is the venom of funnelweb spiders dangerous to humans?

A spider web covered with dew.

**Q.816** Where does a female wolf spider carry her spiderlings?

**Q.817** What shape is an orb web: a square, a rectangle, a triangle, a circle or a parallelogram?

**Q.818** Does a scorpion sting with its claws, its fangs or its tail?

**Q.819** True or false? Centipedes always have 100 legs.

**Q.820** What are marron, yabbies, gilgies and lobbies: beetles, freshwater crays, ticks, mites or dragonflies?

# Australia's Animals (Invertebrates, Frogs, Reptiles)

**Q.821** What is Australia's largest animal-made structure?

**Q.822** Are sponges plants or animals?

**Q.823** True or false? Sponges feed by filtering tiny organisms from water.

**Q.824** Name one marine creature which uses nematocysts to catch food.

Zoanthid polyps have stinging nematocysts on the ends of their tentacles.

**Q.825** True or false? Algae living in the tissues of coral polyps supply their hosts with food materials.

**Q.826** True or false? There are no worms in the ocean.

**Q.827** What are crabs, crays, insects and spiders: reptiles, roundworms, arthropods, mammals or amphibians?

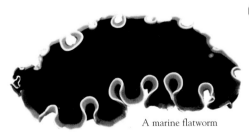

A marine flatworm

A hermit crab looks around.

**Q.828** A crab cannot twist its body. How can it see around it?

**Q.829** What is a Moreton Bay (or Balmain) Bug: a beetle, a marine cray, a centipede, a weevil or a sea jelly?

**Q.830** How many shells has a bivalve mollusc?

**Q.831** Is a frog a vertebrate or an invertebrate?

**Q.832** Do frog eggs have hard shells?

**Q.833** What is the creature which hatches from a frog egg: a pollywog, a sprogget, a tadpole, a grommet or a hush puppy?

**Q.834** How do some Australian frogs survive dry weather?

**Q.835** True or false? All frogs eat plants.

**Q.836** What body feature helps tree-frogs climb slippery surfaces?

**Q.837** Three reptile groups are found in Australia. Snakes and lizards form one group, turtles the second. What is the third group?

**Q.838** What covers the skin of a reptile?

**Q.839** True or false? Reptiles cannot live in dry areas.

A burrowing frog emerging after rain.

**Q.840** Does a reptile move faster or more slowly as its surroundings cool down?

A dragon lizard warming up in the morning sun.

**Q.841** What does a herpetologist study: herpes, hot air balloons, reptiles, sculptures or archery?

**Q.842** How many species of reptile are found in Australia: around 400, around 500, around 600, around 700 or around 800?

**Q.843** Did dinosaurs ever exist in Australia?

**Q.844** What are dinosaurs' closest living relatives: turtles, sharks, fishes, birds or mammals?

**Q.845** Are there any alligators in Australia?

**Q.846** How many species of crocodile live in Australia: one, two, three, four or five?

**Q.847** True or false? The muscles which open a crocodile's mouth are stronger than the muscles which close it.

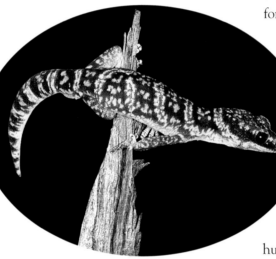

A gecko hunting at night.

A Tiger Snake's venom is deadly to humans.

Saltwater Crocodile

**Q.848** How does a freshwater turtle survive long spells when wetlands dry up?

**Q.849** What does a marine turtle have instead of arms and legs: flippers, floppers, flappers, fluppers or fleppers?

**Q.850** True or false? Five of the seven species of marine turtle occurring in Australian waters are endangered.

**Q.851** True or false? Lizards always have four limbs.

**Q.852** Does a gecko have stiff, hard scales or soft scales?

**Q.853** Can a gecko blink?

**Q.854** True or false? At the first sign of danger, a dragon lizard sheds its tail.

**Q.855** Which long-tailed lizard has strong legs and a forked tongue?

**Q.856** Does a python have a venomous bite?

**Q.857** How do pythons kill their prey?

**Q.858** True or false? Around 20 species of Australian snakes are potentially dangerous to humans.

**Q.859** True or false? Most Australian snakes cannot harm humans.

**Q.860** How does a fish breathe: through its skin, through its lungs, through its book-lungs, through its intestines or through its gills?

A fish takes in water through its mouth, then passes it over its gills.

# Australia's Animals (Fishes, Birds, Mammals)

**Q.861** A Manta Ray may measure 9 m across the disc. Would it eat a human?

**Q.862** Is a shark a fish?

**Q.863** What are two functions of a fish's fins.

**Q.864** True or false? Some fish get food by cleaning pests off the bodies of other fishes.

**Q.865** True or false? The female seahorse hatches her babies in a pouch on her belly.

**Q.866** How does a Lionfish protect itself?

**Q.867** True or false? Anemonefish eat anemone tentacles.

**Q.868** What protects the skins of birds and allows them to fly?

**Q.869** Give three ways in which a bird can use its bill.

This bannerfish has an elongated dorsal fin.

**Q.870** Which of the following birds are flightless: emu, swallow, cassowary, penguin, eagle?

**Q.871** True or false? The bones of flying birds are heavy and solid.

Emu escaping from danger.

**Q.872** How many species of birds have been recorded in Australia and surrounding seas: around 660, around 710, around 760 or around 810?

**Q.873** Do all birds lay eggs?

**Q.874** What grows from the skins of all mammals?

**Q.875** What sort of mammal gives birth to a very undeveloped young one, which is often then reared in a pouch on the mother's belly.

**Q.876** The echidna is a monotreme, an egg-laying mammal. What is the only other monotreme?

**Q.877** A placental mammal keeps its young one in the mother's body until it is well developed. Which two of the following are placental mammals: kangaroo, Dingo, possum, Australian Sea-lion, bandicoot?

**Q.878** What Australian mammals have wings and can fly?

**Q.879** Name three feral mammals that roam the Australian bushland.

**Q.880** What is the status of the Northern Hairy-nosed Wombat, the Bilby and the Bridled Nailtail Wallaby: very common, common, often seen, seldom seen, endangered.

A Lionfish's dorsal fins may inject venom.

A female kangaroo grooming her fur.

**Q.881** True or false? The age of the Earth is approximately 4600 million years.

These limestone Kimberley ranges are the remains of an ancient coral reef.

**Q.882** Grains of zircon estimated to be around 4276 million years old have been found in which Australian State: Queensland, Tasmania or Western Australia?

**Q.883** How long ago was the Kimberley (WA) the site of coral reefs (present today as limestone ranges): 460 million years, 360 million years or 260 million years?

**Q.884** True or false? The oldest rocks in Australia are found in Western Australia.

**Q.885** In Hamelin Pool, Shark Bay, WA, are life-forms called stromatolites, formed by algae. How many millions of years ago did algae like that appear on Earth: 4500, 4000, 3500, 3000 or 2500?

**Q.886** Name a present-day fossil fuel which originated during the Carboniferous period (355–280 million years ago)?

**Q.887** Which emerged on land first, reptiles or amphibians?

**Q.888** Name one present-day amphibian found in Australia.

**Q.889** True or false? Crocodiles existed at the same time as dinosaurs in Australia.

Amphibians were the first vertebrates to emerge from primeval waters.

**Q.890** Where can you see the fossilised bones of the dinosaur *Muttaburrasaurus*: on the Nullarbor Plain, in the Queensland Museum, in the Museum of the Northern Territory or in Nambung National Park?

**Q.891** True or false? Australia was home to huge reptiles such as pliosaurs and ichthyiosaurs, which were not dinosaurs.

**Q.892** True or false? Dinosaurs were present when Australia broke from Antarctica and drifted northwards.

**Q.893** Around how many million years ago did Australia's dinosaurs die out?

**Q.894** True or false? For millions of years Australia drifted across the ocean, far from other continents.

**Q.895** How did small creatures reach Australia as the continent moved nearer to South-east Asia?

**Q.896** Was there ever a land bridge joining Australia to Papua New Guinea?

**Q.897** Between 60 000 and 100 000 years ago, what new arrival in Australia brought change to the whole continent?

**Q.898** Within the past 100 000 years, giant relatives of modern animals lived in Australia. What do we call these creatures: gigafauna, hugeafauna, largerfauna, megafauna or greatafauna?

**Q.899** By 40 000 years ago, humans lived at Lake Mungo, NSW. How has this area changed in the past 40 000 years?

**Q.900** True or false? By 35 000 years ago, humans were living in Tasmania.

Stromatolites in Hamelin Pool Nature Reserve, Shark Bay, WA

An Aboriginal Australian of Australia's Top End painting in a rock gallery

Sea cucumber, also known as beche de mer or trepang

**Q.901** True or false? Australia's indigenous people have never had to survive an Ice Age.

**Q.902** When did the final survivors of the megafauna disappear: 60 000–40 000 years ago or 40 000–20 000 years ago?

**Q.903** Where did Tasmania's Aboriginal people shelter during the Ice Age which ended 13 000 years ago?

**Q.904** What separated Tasmania and the mainland around 12 000 years ago?

**Q.905** What canine animal arrived in northern Australia around 3500 years ago: the fox, the wolf, the Dingo or the jackal?

**Q.906** Did the Aboriginal people form one continuous nation with one language throughout Australia?

**Q.907** True or false? Aboriginal groups did not trade goods.

**Q.908** Why did Aboriginal people in some parts of Australia regularly set fire to old vegetation: to warm themselves, to bring on new grass shoots, to celebrate someone's birthday, to cook food or to drive game animals to hunters?

**Q.909** What do Bogong Moths and Bunya Nuts have in common?

**Q.910** Which of the following was not a purpose for which Aboriginal art was made: to teach, to record events, to signal the presence and history of a group, for sale to visitors?

Top End bushland burning

**Q.911** Were Aboriginal people in greater numbers along the coasts and rivers or in the desert and high mountains?

**Q.912** Give a reason for your answer to Q.911.

**Q.913** In the 1500s, Indonesian (Macassan) people began visiting northern Australia. What were they harvesting: rice, beche de mer (trepang), kangaroo skins, pearls or slaves?

**Q.914** What is beche de mer (trepang): an octopus, a crab, a sea jelly, a sea cucumber or a giant clam?

**Q.915** In 1606, a Dutch ship called the *Duyfken* reached Cape York. Did anyone from the ship land?

**Q.916** What was the Holland-based company which in the 1600s traded in spices, indigo and other South-east Asian products?

**Q.917** True or false? The average Dutch East India Company ship was smaller than today's Manly ferry.

**Q.918** What winds helped Dutch ships sail across the Indian Ocean: the Westerlies, the Easterlies, the Northerlies or the Southerlies?

**Q.919** What did Dutch captain Dirk Hartog leave on an island in Shark Bay, WA, in 1616: a marble headstone, a timber cross, a silver crucifix, a pewter dinner plate or an iron cannon?

**Q.920** Abel Tasman sighted an island he called Van Diemens Land in 1642. What is this island called today?

Dingo howling

Zuytdorp Cliffs, WA, where Dutch East Indiamen might be wrecked in the 1600s.

**Q.921** True or false? No Dutch East India ship was ever wrecked on the coast of WA.

**Q.922** What strait is named after Captain Luis de Torres?

**Q.923** In 1688 and 1699, which English buccaneer visited the coast of Western Australia: William Bligh, William Dampier, William Windsor, William Wordsworth or William Wentworth?

**Q.924** In which year did Captain James Cook sail up the east coast of Australia?

**Q.925** What was the name of Cook's ship: the *Bounty*, the *Endeavour*, the *Investigator*, the *Enterprise* or the *Batavia!*

**Q.926** True or false? Cook did not visit New Zealand.

**Q.927** Which famous botanist (a group of Australian plants is named after him) sailed with Cook?

Statue of Captain James Cook in Hyde Park, Sydney

**Q.928** What link has present-day Melbourne's Fitzroy Gardens with Captain Cook?

**Q.929** Which Queensland cape is near the reef on which the *Endeavour* ran aground?

**Q.930** In 1786, where did the British Government decide to establish a convict settlement: Moreton Bay, Sydney Cove, Roebuck Bay, Botany Bay or Port Phillip?

**Q.931** How many ships were in the First Fleet: 7, 9, 11, 13 or 15?

**Q.932** Were female convicts transported on the First Fleet?

Cadman's Cottage stands in The Rocks, near the site of the first settlement at Sydney Cove.

**Q.933** Where was first settlement eventually made?

**Q.934** Who was the first Governor of the colony at Sydney: Macquarie, Phillip, Bligh, Hunter or King?

**Q.935** True or false? Growing crops in Sydney soil was easy.

**Q.936** Did the British treat the local Aborigines as the rightful custodians of the land around Sydney?

**Q.937** Did Phillip try to establish friendly relations with the Aboriginal people?

**Q.938** After which Aborigine is the land on which today's Opera House stands named?

**Q.939** What name is given to the attempt by the army to take over the colony in 1808: the Brandy Rebellion, the Whisky Rebellion, the Beer Rebellion or the Rum Rebellion?

**Q.940** How did John and Elizabeth Macarthur improve the colony's trade with England?

Sydney Opera House stands on Bennelong Point.

# Timeline Australia

Cliffs in the Blue Mountains, NSW

**Q.941** Flinders and Bass explored Port Jackson in 1795. What was the name of their tiny boat: *Rumpelstiltskin*, *Goldilocks*, *Tom Thumb* or *Cinderella*?

**Q.942** Which mountains did Gregory Blaxland, William Lawson and William Wentworth cross in 1813: the Darling Range, the Blue Mountains, the Stirling Range, the MacDonnell Range or the Australian Alps.

**Q.943** Who was the Aborigine who sailed around Australia with Flinders on the *Investigator*?

**Q.944** Were all the Australian colonies founded in the same year?

**Q.945** Match the State capital with the date of first settlement there: Adelaide, Hobart, Brisbane, Melbourne, Perth: 1803, 1824, 1829, 1835, 1836.

Cobb & Co name on passenger coach.

**Q.946** True or false? In 1850 Port Phillip was separated from New South Wales.

**Q.947** How many convicts arrived in Australia between 1788 and 1868: about 70 000, 100 500, 130 500, 160 500 or 190 000?

**Q.948** What was the last State to use convict labour?

Ned Kelly's armour

**Q.949** Were all the convicts transported to Australia criminals?

**Q.950** What was discovered in the 1850s, bringing great changes to New South Wales and Victoria?

**Q.951** What service did Cobb & Co. provide in Victoria, New South Wales and Queensland from 1853 to 1924?

**Q.952** What are two developments in transport that helped rural Australia?

**Q.953** What name was given to the clash between government forces and goldminers at Ballarat in 1854?

**Q.954** Where did the Kelly Gang make their final stand: Benalla, Jerilderie, Melbourne, Glenrowan or Wagga Wagga?

**Q.955** In the 1800s, what was the name given to someone who settled on land without legal right to do so: a rioter, an explorer, a legislator, a squatter or a loser?

**Q.956** Where were labourers for Queensland's sugar cane farms recruited (or kidnapped) from?

**Q.957** What name was given to these people: Malibus, Diehards, Unionists, Kanakas or Salvationists?

**Q.958** What policy which became a law in 1901 made it difficult for non-Europeans to enter Australia?

**Q.959** What plant pest had overgrown a vast area of Queensland and New South Wales by 1918?

**Q.960** What destroyed this plant: a beetle, a moth larva, a bird, a worm or a weevil?

Convict-built Town Hall, Perth, WA

51

Figures on the National Soldiers War Memorial, Adelaide, SA.

**Q.961** When was gold found in Western Australia: 1852, 1862, 1872, 1882 or 1892?

**Q.962** Where was the Aboriginal resistance leader Jundamurra killed: in the Pilbara, in the Goldfields or in the Kimberley?

**Q.963** What was the original railway between Adelaide and Alice Springs called: the Ghan, Puffing Billy, Old Smokey, the Dead Heart or Rock 'n' Roll?

**Q.964** Which spelling is correct: the Australia Labour Party or the Australian Labor Party?

**Q.965** What political party was born from a meeting of the Australian Workers' Party at Barcaldine, Queensland?

**Q.966** In which State were women first given the vote?

**Q.967** From 1876, what invention made pumping water from the Great Artesian Basin possible?

**Q.968** Who was Jacky Howe: a racehorse, a gun shearer, a politician, a bushranger or a British sailor?

**Q.969** True or false? In the late 1800s, a railway engine could steam from Brisbane to Perth with no problems.

**Q.970** Who was the first woman elected to an Australia parliament: Edith Cavell, Florence Nightingale, Edith Cowan, Enid Lyons or Cheryl Kernot?

This monument to Australians who fought in the Boer War stands in Adelaide, SA.

**Q.971** How many years after the Federation of Australian States did World War I break out?

**Q.972** Did Australians fight in the Boer War (1889-1902)?

**Q.973** True or false? When Britain declared war on Germany in 1914, Australia did so as well.

**Q.974** In which year during World War I did Australian and New Zealand troops mount an assault on Turkish fortifications at Gallipoli: 1914, 1915, 1916, 1917 or 1918?

**Q.975** On what day do Australians remember those who died in times of warfare?

**Q.976** True or false? Between 1941 and 1945, Australia was faced with war in the Pacific.

**Q.977** As a result of World War II, which superpower became Australia's primary ally?

**Q.978** To which country in South-east Asia did Australia send troops between 1962 and 1973?

**Q.979** Were soldiers conscripted to serve in Vietnam?

**Q.980** Is Australia a member of the United Nations?

Anzac Square, Brisbane, Q, is named after the Australian and New Zealand Army Corps.

Mining iron ore in the Pilbara region of Western Australia

**Q.981** True or false? In the late 1990s, Australian soldiers formed part of a UN peacekeeping force in East Timor.

**Q.982** What brought prosperity to Australia in the 1960s: increased cotton production, a minerals boom, better methods of processing fish or fur farms?

**Q.983** When did a referendum give Aborigines the rights of full Australian citizens: 1962, 1963, 1964, 1965 or 1967?

**Q.984** In 1976, what Act gave Aborigines the right to claim vacant or crown land: the Aboriginal Lands Right Act or the Aboriginal Treaty of Rights?

"Greenies" protesting against the proposed damming of the Franklin and Gordon Rivers in Tasmania

**Q.985** Which political party, Liberal or Labor, did each of these Australian Prime Ministers lead: Whitlam, Fraser, Hawke, Keating and Howard?

**Q.986** Which given names match the surnames of the Prime Ministers in Q.985: Paul John, John Winston, Edward Gough, John Malcolm and Robert James.

**Q.987** What are people who do not wish the monarch of England to be Australia's Head of State called: democrats, republicans, autocrats, conservatives or monarchists?

**Q.988** What were these people famous for: Dr John Flynn, Dame Nellie Melba, Sir Donald Bradman and Sir Arthur Streeton?

**Q.989** Did A.B. 'Banjo' Paterson write *The Man from Snowy River*?

**Q.990** What do *Babe*, *My Brilliant Career*, *Mad Max*, *Forty Thousand Horsemen* and *Shine* have in common?

**Q.991** Do the slang terms shonky, hoon, drongo, yobbo and mug lair express approval or disapproval?

**Q.992** The first green ban was imposed by Australian workers in the 1971. What does a green ban try to protect?

**Q.993** If a player wins a Sandover, Brownlow or Phelan Medal, what is his game?

**Q.994** What major sporting event, also held in Sydney, followed the 2000 Sydney Olympics?

**Q.995** What do Gatum Gatum, Toparoa, Van Der Hum, Rogan Josh and Jezabeel have in common?

**Q.996** How did Lloyd Rees, Emily Kame Kngwarreye. Sir Sidney Nolan, Crace Cossington Smith and Sir Hans Heysen express themselves?

**Q.997** What do the initials GST stand for?

**Q.998** In 1999, which country took most Australian exports: Taiwan, Japan, Korean, the USA or New Zealand?

**Q.999** What is the average number of children for Australian families: 0.77, 1.77, 2.77 or 3.77?

**Q.1000** What is the life expectancy for a girl born in 1999: 75-80 years, 80-85 years, 85-90 years.

The life expectancy of this child should be more than 80 years.

Australia's Coat of Arms

## AUSTRALIA - GENERAL
### Pages 4 to 7

1 The Australian dollar ($A).
2 No.
3 The Superb Lyrebird.
4 Blue, red, yellow.
5 The Outback.
6 Around the coast.
7 About 19 million.
8 True.
9 New South Wales, Queensland, South Australia, Tasmania, Victoria, Western Australia (States); Australian Capital Territory and Northern Territory (Territories).
10 In Canberra.
11 Yes.
12 Queen Elizabeth II, represented by the Governor-General of Australia.
13 1 January, 1901.
14 ATSIC.
15 South land.
16 No.
17 They are all External Territories of Australia.
18 Someone of Aboriginal or Torres Strait Islander descent; an original inhabitant of Australia (either).
19 True.
20 A lower House of Representatives and an upper House of Assembly (except for Queensland, which has no Upper House).
21 The Prime Minister.
22 A Minister
23 False. It is the oldest.
24 South Australia.
25 18.
26 6.
27 As a sign of mourning.
28 True.
29 Black, yellow and red.
30 The yellow circle represents the Sun, on a field of black (the night sky) and red (the earth).

31 *Age* – Melbourne, *Courier Mail* – Brisbane, *Mercury* – Hobart, *West Australian* – Perth.
32 Vegemite.
33 "God save our gracious Queen". It is used in the presence of the Queen or a member of the royal family.
34 Advance Australia Fair.
35 The Golden Wattle.
36 They are all past Prime Ministers of Australia.
37 The Constitution.
38 False. The majority of YES votes must be in a majority of States.
39 Emu and Red Kangaroo.
40 Yes.
41 Southern.
42 Indian Ocean, Southern Ocean, Pacific Ocean, Arafura Sea.
43 Bass Strait.
44 True.
45 Papua New Guinea.
46 7 682 300 km².
47 Three.
48 24 times.
49 East-west.
50 False.
51 The Tropic of Capricorn.
52 False. Queensland does not observe Eastern Summer Time.
53 The Great Barrier Reef
54 Alice Springs.
55 53.1°C.
56 Charlotte Pass.
57 Lake Eyre, South Australia.
58 Cape York.
59 Ocean currents.
60 Dry.
61 Any two of: Kakadu National Park, Uluru–Kata Tjuta National Park (NT); Riversleigh/Naracoorte Fossil Sites (Q/SA); Great Barrier Reef, Wet Tropics, Fraser I. (Q); East Coast Temperate and Sub-temperate Rainforest Parks (Q/NSW); Greater Blue Mountains, Willandra Lakes, Lord Howe Island Group (NSW); Tasmanian Wilderness (T); Shark Bay (WA).
62 True.
63 They all originated in Australia.
64 False. It was introduced into Australia from Hawaii.
65 False. The Western Plateau covers most of the western side of the continent.

66 The Murray River.
67 Sydney, New South Wales.
68 Darwin.
69 Sydney, Melbourne, Brisbane, Perth, Hobart.
70 Canberra, Australian Capital Territory.
71 Commonwealth Scientific and Industrial Research Organisation.
72 False. Australia's highest mountains are in the Great Dividing Range, in the south-east of the continent.
73 North–south.
74 On the eastern side.
75 Darwin is the capital of a Territory, not a State.
76 Sydney.
77 1861.
78 Michael Jordan.
79 True.
80 They were artists who painted pictures.

## NEW SOUTH WALES
### Pages 8 to 11

Sydney Opera House

81 False.
82 801 600 km².
83 Yes.
84 Queensland on the north, South Australia on the west and Victoria on the south.
85 The Great Dividing Range.
86 False. Sydney, not Melbourne, is the capital of New South Wales.
87 The Waratah.
88 Around 6 million.
89 Lion and kangaroo.
90 Mt Kosciuszko
91 The Platypus.
92 Sydney (3 986 723), Newcastle (567 302), Wollongong (380 660), Wagga Wagga (56 566), Broken Hill (21 297).

93 In 1788.
94 Convicts.
95 The Sydney Opera House.
96 Captain Arthur Phillip.
97 Elizabeth and John Macarthur.
98 The Blue Mountains.
99 In 1850.
100 True.
101 Sandstone.
102 1879.
103 True.
104 The AMP Tower at Centrepoint is the tallest building in the Southern Hemisphere.
105 True.
106 Taronga.
107 The Olympic Games.
108 Cape Byron Lighthouse.
109 In summer, NSW observes Daylight Saving, while Queensland does not.
110 The Queensland/New South Wales border.
111 West.
112 The Jenolan Caves.
113 The Three Sisters.
114 Wine.
115 Country.
116 Gemstones.
117 True.
118 Scarborough and Cottesloe are beaches near Perth, WA.
119 National parks on the northern coastline of New South Wales.
120 In 1932.
121 False. Parkes is a centre for astronomers who study the heavens.
122 Sugar and bananas.
123 False.
124 Opal.
125 True.
126 The Great Artesian Basin.
127 A long way from the city.
128 The New England Tableland.
129 Henry Parkes.
130 It is a popular location for films and TV productions.
131 They live underground.
132 Arid.
133 Sand dunes.
134 The Riverina or Murrumbidgee Irrigation Area (either).
135 Copper, zinc, lead, silver (any one).
136 Gold.

137 Dubbo.
138 The Darling and the Murray Rivers.
139 Wodonga.
140 The Murray Cod.
141 Sir Donald Bradman.
142 A blowhole.
143 Buddhism.
144 "Sound of the sea".
145 The Southern Highlands are at higher altitude than the coastal plain where Wollongong is situated.
146 A town.
147 Whales.
148 Cheese.
149 Fishing.
150 True.
151 Eastern Grey Kangaroos.
152 True. Jervis Bay is the outlet to the sea for the Australian Capital Territory.
153 The Murray River.
154 Kosciuszko National Park.
155 False. He was a young stationhand.
156 The first European to climb it, in 1840, was the Polish Count Paul de Strzelecki.
157 2228 m.
158 19.
159 They are all winter sports resorts (ski resorts).
160 Trout.

## VICTORIA
### Pages 12 to 15

Flinders Street Station, Melbourne

161 The Garden State.
162 The Common Heath.
163 Melbourne, Geelong, Ballarat, Bendigo, Shepparton.
164 South-eastern.
165 False. Tasmania is the smallest Australian State.

166 227 600 km².
167 The five stars of the Southern Cross.
168 Just under 5 million (4 736 815).
169 The Yarra River.
170 The south bank.
171 Angel.
172 Melbourne Cricket Ground.
173 True
174 Second-largest.
175 False. The cottage in Fitzroy Gardens was the home of the parents of Captain James Cook.
176 November.
177 True.
178 Flinders Street Station.
179 A glass cone.
180 Australian Rules.
181 Westgate Bridge.
182 1886.
183 Moomba.
184 Port Phillip Bay.
185 Eastern.
186 True.
187 The ocean cross-currents at the entrance to Port Phillip Bay.
188 False. The island can be reached by bridge or by ferry.
189 Australian Fur-seals.
190 Little Penguin.
191 Puffing Billy.
192 50 km.
193 Native.
194 The Platypus.
195 True.
196 Yes.
197 Brown coal.
198 90 Mile Beach.
199 Yes.
200 A half-stone creature of Aboriginal legend.
201 Sir George Gipps.
202 Leadbeater's Possum.
203 False. It is Victoria's largest reserve.
204 The High Country.
205 Mt Bogong (1986 m).
206 True.
207 Bushwalking, fishing, rock-climbing, horseback-riding. birdwatching, canoeing, waterskiing, sailing (any three).
208 June.
209 Gold.
210 At the Eureka Stockade.

211 They were all gold-mining towns.

212 Castlemaine XXXX.

213 The world's richest sprint footrace, the Stawell Gift (120 m) is held at Stawell.

214 The Kelly Gang: Ned and Dan Kelly, Joe Byrne and Steve Hart.

215 More than 2500 km.

216 False. Lake Alexandrina is in South Australia, not Victoria.

217 The water flow is lessening, locks and weirs hold up the flow and trees along the course have been cut down (any two).

218 A boat impelled by paddlewheels driven by a steam engine.

219 Carrying passengers and freight.

220 False. Paddlesteamers now carry tourists and holiday-makers.

221 Albury-Wodonga, Echuca, Swan Hill, Robinvale, Mildura.

222 The Murray River.

223 Southern.

224 South Australia.

225 The Mallee.

226 False. A mallee is a eucalypt with a number of short trunks growing from one large root.

227 Sand.

228 The Wimmera.

229 Rock-climbing.

230 True.

231 Sheep.

232 Coastal.

233 Warrnambool and Anglesea.

234 Limestone stacks left standing in the sea in Port Campbell National Park.

235 True.

236 They were ships wrecked off Victoria's south-west coast in the 1800s.

237 High.

238 False. Bells Beach is the scene of an annual surfing contest.

239 Port Phillip Bay.

240 Geelong.

## TASMANIA
### Pages 16 to 18

241 Sea levels rose after an Ice Age ended.

242 False. Aboriginal people may have been in Tasmania for more than 35 000 years.

243 The Thylacine (Tasmanian Tiger).

Richmond Bridge, Tasmania

244 No. It is probably extinct.

245 Mt Ossa (1617 m).

246 The Tasmanian Blue Gum.

247 True.

248 In caves.

249 False. There are many Tasmanians of Aboriginal descent.

250 Least.

251 More than 3 m.

252 Abel Tasman.

253 Van Diemen's Land.

254 France.

255 Sealing or whaling (either).

256 True.

257 The Derwent.

258 Launceston.

259 Launceston.

260 False. They were hardened re-offenders.

261 Mt Wellington.

262 It was rammed by a cargo ship.

263 Built 1823–25, it is the oldest bridge in Australia.

264 The Huon Pine.

265 Daintree.

266 Electricity generated by moving water.

267 To provide hydro-electricity.

268 Port Arthur.

269 More than 1800 convicts lie buried there in unmarked graves.

270 Savage dogs were chained across 100-metre-wide Eaglehawk Neck and sharks abound in the local sea.

271 False. There are ruins and many other relics.

272 A paving-like rock formation at Pirates Bay, Tasman Peninsula.

273 Because of its shape.

274 Ice.

275 Yes.

276 False. It is held annually.

277 South Cape.

278 True.

279 The Sun Coast.

280 A black and white marsupial now found only in Tasmania.

281 Bicheno.

282 France.

283 A mountain range.

284 Bananas and sugar cane.

285 Morphine.

286 Devonport.

287 True.

288 The plug of an extinct volcano, which rises 152 m.

289 True.

290 All seven are mined in Tasmania.

291 Copper.

292 A giant heath (a plant).

293 More than 200 m.

294 Ice (or glaciers).

295 Farming animals which live in salt or fresh water.

296 Atlantic salmon, abalone, crayfish, scallops, oysters (any one).

297 Yes.

298 They are the peaks of mountains drowned by rising sea level.

299 King and Flinders Islands.

300 Dairy products (especially cheese and cream).

## SOUTH AUSTRALIA
### Pages 19 to 21

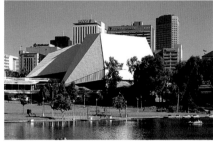
Torrens River, Adelaide

301 The third-largest (NT is not a State).

302 Sturt's Desert Pea.

303 The Australian Magpie.

304 The Southern Hairy-nosed Wombat.

305 False. It is concentrated in the south-east corner of the State.

306 True.

307 Lake Eyre.

308 False. South Australia is the driest State.

309 Cool and wet.

310 St Vincent Gulf.

311 The Mt Lofty Ranges.

312 The Torrens River.

313 1836.

314 False. It was founded as a colony of free settlers.

315 Colonel William Light was the Surveyor-General who planned Adelaide.

316 Every two years.

317 A world music festival.

318 False. Rundle Mall is a pedestrian thoroughfare.

319 Maslins was the first official nude beach in Australia.

320 Grapes, citrus fruits and almonds.

321 Port Adelaide.

322 Eastern.

323 German (or Prussian, or Silesian).

324 Hahndorf.

325 Wine.

326 Mt Woodroffe (1439 m).

327 It provides most of the State's water.

328 Gliding.

329 Lake Alexandrina.

330 A long, narrow coastal lagoon stretching about 145 km from the Murray mouth.

331 Fossils of prehistoric animals.

332 Blue.

333 True.

334 Cave divers.

335 Eastern.

336 Lobster, crayfish, prawn, shrimp (any two).

337 North.

338 True.

339 A large crater (or amphitheatre, basin or bowl) in the ranges.

340 Sir Donald Campbell set a world land-speed record of 648.6 kph (1040 mph) in the jet-powered car *Bluebird*.

341 False. Lake Eyre may fill with water four times in 100 years.

342 It flows through a network of rivers and creeks after very heavy rain.

343 Yes.

344 Opal.

345 They live underground.

346 True.

347 Uranium and copper.

348 11.

349 Iron ore.

350 False. Ship-building at Whyalla ceased in 1978.

351 Tuna.

352 1100 km.

353 False. It is bordered by steep limestone cliffs and narrow beaches.

354 No trees.

355 Limestone.

356 No.

357 Lichen.

358 The Australian Sea-lion.

359 The Great White Shark (or White Pointer Shark).

360 Southern Right Whales.

## WESTERN AUSTRALIA
### Pages 22 to 25

Perth city, Western Australia

361 One-third

362 West Cape Howe is WA's most southerly point, Cape Londonderry its most northerly.

363 True.

364 The Gascoyne.

365 Perth, Fremantle, Boulder/Kalgoorlie, Geraldton, Albany.

366 The Red and Green Kangaroo Paw.

367 The Black Swan.

368 Termites.

369 Mt Augustus.

370 True.

371 Two Red Kangaroos.

372 Fremantle and Perth.

373 Perth.

374 1829.

375 True.

376 They are all beaches near Perth.

377 To see the wildflowers.

378 20 minutes.

379 Small wallabies.

380 In winter.

381 At Walpole.

382 (The Department of) Conservation And Land Management.

383 True.

384 False. Perth stands on a sandplain.

385 The Karri.

386 True.

387 Wine.

388 The Bussell family.

389 On the coast.

390 Cape Leeuwin.

391 Dutch and French.

392 Big trees.

393 Rice and pineapples.

394 False. Torndirrup is noted for granite headlands and sandy beaches.

395 Albany.

396 Whaling.

397 A range of mountains.

398 A rocky outcrop.

399 Granite.

400 Sheep.

401 Gold.

402 Yes.

403 By pipeline from Mundaring, near Perth.

404 Wide.

405 North.

406 The Pinnacles.

407 Tree roots and trunks.

408 A Benedictine (Catholic) monastery.

409 Rock lobster.

410 Low islands off the coast near Geraldton.

411 The *Batavia*.

412 The Murchison.

413 Stone.

414 A Dutch sailing ship wrecked there in 1629.

415 An inscribed pewter plate.

416 Yes.

417 False. Shark Bay is 840 km north of Perth.

418 Tomatoes, bananas, beans.

419 Arid.

420 True.

421 Bottle-nosed Dolphins.

422 Yes.

423 They are descendants of ancient forms of life present on Earth 3500 million years ago.

424 True.

425 Twice the size.

426 Iron ore.
427 Karijini.
428 Dampier.
429 Very hot in summer.
430 Ningaloo.
431 The Kimberley (Kimberley Division).
432 In summer.
433 Broome.
434 True.
435 Ancient coral reefs.
436 Diamonds.
437 Made.
438 Cone-shaped, orange-and-black striped mountains in the East Kimberley.
439 True.
440 It is swollen.

## NORTHERN TERRITORY
Pages 26 to 29

Uluṟu rising from the wildflower-covered plain

441 Sturt's Desert Rose.
442 Timor and Arafura Seas, Gulf of Carpentaria.
443 True.
444 The Top End.
445 Because its sand and rocks are mainly reddish in colour.
446 The Victoria.
447 The Monsoon.
448 The Wet (or The Green).
449 Common.
450 The Wedge-tailed Eagle.
451 Darwin.
452 True.
453 64.
454 Cyclone Tracy
455 Fish.
456 The Saltwater Crocodile.
457 All three.
458 Because of stinging jellyfish.

459 To watch birds.
460 Around its neck.
461 Leap from the water.
462 East.
463 The Gagudju.
464 False.
465 At least 40 000 years.
466 The edge of a plateau (edge of a tableland).
467 Albatross and gannet.
468 Mining.
469 Uranium.
470 A crocodile.
471 Insects ("white ants").
472 Because they are oriented north-south.
473 In the north-east.
474 An island (in the Gulf of Carpentaria).
475 A cattle station.
476 Yes.
477 The Stuart Highway.
478 The Katherine.
479 Katherine.
480 Thermal springs.
481 *We of the Never-Never.*
482 1508 km.
483 False.
484 Large, rounded, granite boulders.
485 The Barkly Tableland.
486 Stuart.
487 The Todd.
488 The boats have no bottoms. The Todd is dry and competitors run along the sand with them.
489 True.
490 The Royal Flying Doctor Service.
491 The MacDonnell Ranges.
492 South.
493 An ancestor of the Dreaming (the gecko ancestor, Itirkawara).
494 Garnets.
495 The Larapinta Trail.
496 Ochre.
497 False. For most of the time these rivers are dry.
498 Simpsons Gap.
499 White.
500 Palms (*Livistona* palms).
501 Kings Canyon.
502 False. The name comes from the red and gold tones of the valley cliffs.
503 470 km.

504 False.
505 No. Mt Augustus in WA is bigger.
506 True.
507 Yulara.
508 The traditional Aboriginal custodians of Uluṟu.
509 No.
510 Nearly 350 m.
511 A number of domes.
512 Higher.
513 Sandstone.
514 Queensland, Western Australia and South Australia.
515 True.
516 Yes. Wildflowers are seen after rain.
517 In the south-eastern corner.
518 The Tanami.
519 The Dingo.
520 True.

## QUEENSLAND
Pages 30 to 33

The beach at South Bank Parklands

521 20%.
522 The Cooktown Orchid.
523 True.
524 3.5 million.
525 Three.
526 Camerons Corner.
527 True.
528 The Koala.
529 The Brolga.
530 "Bold but faithful".
531 Brisbane, Gold Coast/Tweed, Townsville, Cairns, Mount Isa.
532 Tully.
533 Brisbane.
534 True.
535 The Brisbane River.
536 True.
537 On the south bank.

Moored craft, Whitsunday Islands

538 October–March.

539 True.

540 At Mt Coot-tha.

541 60 minutes.

542 The Tweed River.

543 Rainbow Lorikeets and Scaly-breasted Lorikeets (either).

544 Dolphins, seals or Killer Whales (any one).

545 They are all associated with the Gold Coast.

546 False. It was named after the colour of its sand.

547 Yes.

548 Queensland and New South Wales.

549 Subtropical.

550 Sand dunes and sandstone domes.

551 False. It was the scene of intense volcanic activity.

552 The Bruce Highway.

553 The Glass House Mountains.

554 False. The Sunshine Coast is just north of Brisbane.

555 They are towns on the Sunshine Coast.

556 Inland.

557 Pineapples, sugar cane and avocados.

558 It is the world's largest sand island (or it is made entirely of sand).

559 200 m.

560 Yes.

561 Whale-watching.

562 Humpback Whales.

563 Raine Island.

564 True.

565 Yes.

566 True.

567 1981.

568 If water temperatures rise above the upper limit for the growth of coral, the reef will die.

569 They are Great Barrier Reef islands.

570 Bauxite.

571 Rockhampton.

572 Beef.

573 True.

574 Hiring a boat to sail.

575 False. It is the third-largest city.

576 Castle Hill.

577 Magnetic Island.

578 Cardwell.

579 False. All the island is national park.

580 Whitewater rafting.

581 Trinity Inlet.

582 False.

583 Kuranda.

584 Rainforest.

585 The Atherton Tableland.

586 Oats.

587 True.

588 No. It includes areas from Townsville to Cooktown.

589 Captain James Cook.

590 Approximately 950 km.

591 Thursday Island (or Prince of Wales Island).

592 Westwards.

593 The Darling Downs.

594 A wine- and fruit-growing area.

595 True.

596 The Great Artesian Basin.

597 The south-west.

598 Around 100.

599 Copper, silver, lead and zinc.

600 Limestone at Riversleigh contains many fossils of prehistoric animals.

## AUSTRALIAN CAPITAL TERRITORY

### Pages 34 to 36

601 True.

602 False. Robert Campbell established a sheep station there in 1825.

603 Duntroon.

604 1860.

605 1911.

606 It is halfway between rival cities, Sydney and Melbourne.

607 Melbourne.

608 False. It occupies .03% of Australia.

609 The Murrumbidgee.

610 Bimberi Peak.

611 Jervis Bay.

612 35 km.

613 A meeting place.

614 Walter Burley Griffin.

615 False. Burley Griffin was an American, from Chicago.

616 1920.

617 The Molonglo, a tributary of the Murrumbidgee.

618 1964.

619 The Gang-gang Cockatoo.

620 True.

621 Royal Bluebell.

622 One is black and one is white.

623 Yes.

624 True.

625 True.

626 1989.

627 The Australian (Federal) Parliament; the ACT Parliament (either).

628 The House of Representatives and the Senate.

629 1927.

630 1988.

631 Capital Hill.

632 True.

633 Yes.

634 4500.

635 False. The mosaic is based on an Aboriginal design.

636 One.

637 36 km.

638 Captain Cook.

639 137 m.

640 30%.

641 Black Mountain.

Mosaic forecourt, Parliament House, Canberra

642 195.2 m.

643 Australian Institute of Sport.

644 1981.

645 Yes.

646 Works of art.

647 Questacon

648 Japan.

649 The Army.

650 Anzac Avenue

651 The Unknown Soldier.

652 Captain Cook.

653 Lake Burley Griffin.

654 Floriade.

655 False. In Autumn, the leaves of deciduous trees change colour before falling.

656 Plants.

657 True.

658 True.

659 Tidbinbilla Deep Space Communications Complex is operated by Australia for the US space agency NASA.

660 Namadgi.

**AUSTRALIA'S LANDFORMS**
**Pages 37 to 40**

Water wears away rock.

661 Up to 100 km.

662 Thicker.

663 Molten rock from the Earth's interior.

664 True.

665 Yes.

666 Around 4300 million years b.p.

667 Gondwana (Gondwanaland).

668 Antarctica.

669 Yes.

670 Mountains.

671 Buckling of the Earth's crust.

672 True.

673 By the cooling of magma forced to the Earth's surface.

674 True.

675 Granite, basalt and pumice.

676 Molten rock ejected from a volcano.

677 Magma forcing its way to the surface through vents or cracks.

678 The traces of some life-form preserved as stone, footprints or imprints.

679 Naracoorte (SA), Riversleigh (Q), caves on the Nullarbor Plain (WA, SA) and Dinosaur Cove (V).

680 Fossil plants and animals of the same sort have been found in all three.

681 Strata

682 The heat of the Earth's interior.

683 True.

684 Wind, water, ice, temperature changes, gravity, chemical changes (any three).

685 Some elements in the rock expand and contract at a different rate from others when heated or cooled. This causes cracking.

686 False.

687 Their roots and stems grow and split the rock, and they produce chemicals which act on rock (either).

688 True.

689 Hastens it.

690 True.

691 A "river" of ice, fed by snowfall, which moves very slowly downhill.

692 False. Around 280 million years ago, half of Australia was covered by glaciers.

693 By ice.

694 U-shaped.

695 Billabong.

696 A delta.

697 When its flow slows down.

698 At the foot of a waterfall.

699 True.

700 In south-eastern Australia.

701 1300 m.

702 Antarctica.

703 No.

704 13 000.

705 Mt Warning.

706 By volcanic eruptions.

707 True.

708 They were all formed by volcanos (or by volcanic action).

709 As "blue metal" for road construction.

710 They are all made of granite.

711 False. Diamonds, rubies, garnets, sapphires and zircons are all brought to the surface by volcanic action.

712 Sedimentary rock.

713 Sandstone.

714 False.

715 A pound.

716 Faults.

717 An anticline.

718 Decayed vegetation (plants).

719 Vegetable.

720 Bass Strait, off Victoria, and the north-west coast of Western Australia.

721 True.

722 Jasper.

723 Sand.

724 A hard layer of rock which caps softer rocks.

725 Mesa, butte, tableland and plateau.

726 A plain covered with small stones.

727 Fast.

728 Stalagmites go up, stalactites go down.

729 The Jenolan Caves.

730 True.

731 False.

732 Water: rivers, creeks, waterways.

733 The limestone is the remains of ancient coral reefs.

734 True.

735 No.

736 Swash.

737 These cities are all sited on river estuaries.

738 Yes.

739 10 m.

740 Wave action.

**AUSTRALIA'S PLANTS**
**Pages 41 to 43**

741 Fungi and lichens.

742 Fungi.

743 True.

744 Sunshine.

745 Necessary.

746 Green or black.

747 True.

748 Yes.

Flowering plants developed comparatively recently.

**749** Cellulose.

**750** True.

**751** Sap.

**752** Wood.

**753** Soft stems.

**754** Towards light.

**755** No.

**756** Bark.

**757** They take in water and dissolved minerals; they anchor the plant in place (either).

**758** A shrub is smaller than a tree (less than 2 m tall).

**759** Yes.

**760** A weed.

**761** True.

**762** Seaweeds.

**763** Yes.

**764** With bladders (floats).

**765** Blue-green algae.

**766** True.

**767** Plankton.

**768** False. Ferns are a very ancient form of plant life.

**769** Damp.

**770** By spores.

**771** A pine tree.

**772** True.

**773** They are all conifers (pine trees).

**774** In the Blue Mountains.

**775** Most recent.

**776** Reproductive.

**777** True.

**778** They eat the nectar, which has a high energy value.

**779** True.

**780** A seed.

**781** By petal shape, petal colour, scent and texture (any two).

**782** Flying-fox, butterfly, Honey-possum and bee.

**783** True.

**784** On the wind.

**785** Yes.

**786** A fruit.

**787** Gumnuts.

**788** Far from the parent plant.

**789** By wind, by water, being being carried on an animal or by mechanical means such as catapulting or springing (any two).

**790** The Mountain Ash.

**791** 150 m.

**792** 2500 years.

**793** Sundews and pitcher plants.

**794** Eucalypts.

**795** The Boab (in Africa, the Baobab).

**796** False. In 1788, around 10% of Australia was covered by forests.

**797** Sir Joseph Banks.

**798** Charles Sturt (Sturt's Desert Pea and Sturt's Desert Rose).

**799** True.

**800** The hollows in which they sleep and breed appear only in old trees.

## AUSTRALIA'S ANIMALS

### Pages 44 to 47

**801** An invertebrate animal has no backbone; a vertebrate has a backbone (made up of vertebrae).

**802** True.

**803** Invertebrates.

**804** Outside.

**805** Housefly, crab and centipede.

**806** 3.

**807** True.

**808** True.

**809** Flies, mosquitoes, bugs, fleas, sandflies, gnats, lice (any two).

**810** The Bogong Moth.

**811** Four.

**812** True.

**813** False. A spider breathes through book-lungs.

**814** No.

**815** Yes.

**816** On her back.

**817** A circle.

**818** With the tip of its tail.

**819** False. They rarely have as many as 100 legs.

**820** Freshwater crays.

**821** The Great Barrier Reef, made by tiny coral polyps.

**822** Animals.

**823** True.

**824** Sea jellies, sea anemones, coral polyps, hydroids, bluebottles, zoanthid polyps (any one).

**825** True.

**826** False

**827** They are all arthropods.

**828** Its eyes are on stalks which can swivel around.

**829** A marine cray.

**830** Two.

**831** A vertebrate.

**832** No.

**833** A tadpole.

**834** They burrow or hide in a hole and go into summer sleep mode (aestivate).

**835** False. Frogs eat small creatures.

**836** Their fingers and toes end in adhesive discs.

**837** Crocodiles.

**838** Scales.

**839** False.

A female kangaroo grooming her fur

Anemonefish sheltering in a sea anemone

840 More slowly.
841 Reptiles.
842 Around 700.
843 Yes.
844 Birds.
845 No.
846 Two.
847 False. The muscles that close a crocodiles mouth are very powerful.
848 It buries itself in the ground.
849 Flippers.
850 True.
851 False. According to species, a lizard may have no, two or four limbs.
852 Soft scales.
853 No. Its lower, transparent eyelids are fused to its upper lids.
854 False. A dragon lizard cannot shed its tail naturally.
855 A monitor (goanna).
856 No.
857 Pythons kill their prey by squeezing it so the animal cannot breathe.
858 True.
859 True.
860 Through gills.
861 No. It eats plankton (tiny marine animals and plants).
862 Yes.
863 A fish may use its fins to swim, to dig holes in sand, to fan water over eggs, to inject venom into attackers, to send signals to other fish, to court other fish (any two).
864 True.
865 False. The male seahorses hatches his babies in a pouch on his belly.

866 Spines on its back fins can inject venom into an attacker.
867 False. Anemonefish (also known as clownfish) shelter amongst anemone tentacles.
868 Feathers.
869 To peck up food, to preen its feathers, to preen another bird, to drink water, to peck out a nest site, to carry nesting material, to catch prey (any three).
870 Emu, cassowary and penguin.
871 False. The bones of flying birds are light and hollow.
872 Around 760.
873 Yes.
874 Hair or fur.
875 A marsupial.
876 The Platypus.
877 Dingo and Australian Sea-lion.
878 Bats and flying-foxes (either).
879 Cat, camel, buffalo, donkey, horse, dog, deer, pig (any three).
880 They are endangered.

## TIMELINE AUSTRALIA
### Pages 48 to 53

An Aboriginal Australian of Australia's Top End

881 True.
882 Western Australia.

883 360 million years.
884 True.
885 3500 million years.
886 Coal, or petroleum oil.
887 Amphibians.
888 Frog or cane toad.
889 True.
890 In the Queensland Museum.
891 True.
892 False. Dinosaurs disappeared before Australia finally broke away from Antarctica.
893 65 million years ago.
894 True.
895 They flew (bats and birds) or drifted on floating debris (rats, mice, reptiles).
896 No.
897 The arrival of the first humans, whose descendants are the present day indigenous Australians.
898 Megafauna.
899 It has become much drier and is now desert.
900 True.
901 False. The latest Ice Age was at its height 18 000 years ago, and ended 13 000 years ago.
902 40 000–20 000 years ago.
903 In caves.
904 Rising sea levels caused by melting of ice.
905 The Dingo.
906 No. They lived in many groups, in different locations, with different languages and cultures.
907 False. They traded goods over long distances.
908 To bring on new grass shoots and to drive game to hunters (either one).
909 They were seasonal foods harvested by several groups of Aboriginal people.
910 For sale to visitors.
911 Along the coast and rivers.
912 These areas had more food and shelter.
913 Beche de mer (trepang).
914 A species of sea cucumber that is used in Asian cooking.
915 Yes. The ship's carpenter raised a flag.
916 The Dutch East India Company.
917 True. It was around 50 m long, compared with a Manly ferry's 70.4 m.

918 The Westerlies.

919 A pewter plate.

920 Tasmania.

921 False. Many sailed too far east and were wrecked on the coast of Western Australia.

922 Torres Strait.

923 William Dampier.

924 1770.

925 The *Endeavour*.

926 False. He sailed around New Zealand.

927 Joseph (later Sir Joseph) Banks.

928 His parents' cottage and a statue of him stand in the gardens.

929 Cape Tribulation.

930 Botany Bay.

931 11.

932 Yes.

933 Sydney Cove (or Port Jackson or Sydney Harbour).

934 Captain Arthur Phillip.

935 False.

936 No.

937 Yes.

938 Bennelong.

939 The Rum Rebellion.

940 They improved the quality of the colony's wool by crossing Spanish Merinos with coarse-woolled sheep.

941 The *Tom Thumb*.

942 The Blue Mountains.

943 Bungaree.

944 No.

945 Hobart 1803, Brisbane 1824, Perth 1829, Melbourne 1835, Adelaide 1836.

946 True.

947 About 160 500.

948 Western Australia.

949 No. Some were convicted of political activities against the British Government.

950 The discovery of gold.

951 Cobb & Co. horse-drawn coach service.

952 The establishment of roads, the spread of railways, the use of paddlesteamers and the use of light aircraft (any two).

953 Eureka Stockade.

954 Glenrowan.

955 A squatter.

956 The Pacific islands.

957 Kanakas.

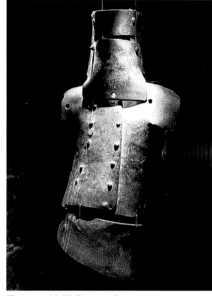

The armour Ned Kelly wore at his capture

958 The White Australia Policy.

959 The Prickly Pear.

960 A moth larva, *Cactoblastis cactorum*.

961 1892.

962 The Kimberley.

963 The Ghan, after the Afghan camel drivers who had previously travelled the route with freight.

964 The Australian Labor Party.

965 The Australian Labor Party.

966 In South Australia in 1894.

967 An inexpensive windmill.

968 A gun shearer.

969 False. States had different widths between tracks (gauges) so engines and carriages had to be changed.

970 Edith Cowan.

971 13.

972 Yes.

973 True.

974 1915.

975 On Anzac Day (25 April).

976 True.

977 The United States of America.

978 Vietnam.

979 Yes.

980 Yes.

981 True.

982 A minerals boom.

983 1967.

984 The Aboriginal Land Rights Act.

985 Whitlam, Hawke and Keating led Labor, Fraser and Howard the Liberal Party.

986 John Winston Howard, Edward Gough Whitlam, John Malcolm Fraser, Paul John Keating, Robert James Hawke.

987 Republicans.

988 Dr John Flynn: Royal Flying Doctor Service; Dame Nellie Melba: opera (soprano); Sir Donald Bradman: cricket; and Sir Arthur Streeton: fine art (painting).

989 Yes.

990 They are Australian-made films.

991 Disapproval.

992 The environment (green spaces, significant buildings).

993 Australian Rules Football.

994 The Sydney Paralympic Games.

995 They are the names of racehorses that won the Melbourne Cup.

996 They were artists who painted pictures.

997 Goods and Services Tax.

998 Japan.

999 1.77.

1000 80-85 years.

Figures on the National Soldiers War Memorial, Adelaide

# Index to illustrations

Aboriginal Australian  48, 62
Adelaide  52, 56
Adelaide River  27
Albany  23
amphibian  48
AMP Tower, Centrepoint  8
anemonefish  62
Angel  12
Anzac Square  52
Arthur Range  17
Ash, Mountain  43
Banksia, Scarlet  43
bannerfish  47
bark  41
beche de mer  49
Beer Can Regatta  26
beetle  44
Bennelong Point  50
Birdsville Hotel  33
Blue Mountains  51
Blundell's Farmhouse  34
Boab tree  25
Boer War memorial  52
Botanic Gardens, Mt Coot-tha  30
Brisbane  52
Brisbane River  30
Broome, camel-riding at  25
Bungle Bungles, the  25
butterflies  44
Cadman's Cottage  50
Cairns  33
Canberra  34, 35, 36
Cape York  6
Capital Hill  35
Carnarvon Ranges  33
Chambers Pillars  28
child  53
City Beach  22
coastline, Australian  6
Coat of Arms, Australian  5, 54
Cobb & Co. coach  51
Cockatoo, Gang-gang  34
Cook, Captain James  50
   Memorial Water Jet  35
crab, hermit  45
Crocodile, Saltwater  27, 46
Dandenongs  13
Darwin, NT  7
Derwent River  16
Devil, Tasmanian  17
Devils Marbles  28
Dingo  29, 49
Dolphins, Bottlenose  25

dune  40
Duntroon  34
Eagle, Wedge-tailed  26
Emu  47
Eureka Stockade, replica  14
Federation Peak  40
ferns  42
fish  46
flag, Australian  5
flatworm, marine  45
Flinders Street Station  12, 55
Flinders Ranges  20
Floriade  36
fossil fern leaves  37
Freshwater Cray, Lamington  44
Freycinet National Park  18
frog, burrowing  45
fruits, eucalypt  43
gecko  46
Geikie Gorge  40
Ghost Gum  28
gibbers  40
Glass House Mountains  31
Gold Coast  31
Grampians  15
Great Australian Bight  21
Great Barrier Reef  6, 32
Great Dividing Range  7
"Greenies"  53
Hazards  18
Hobart  16
House of Representatives, Federal  5
Hyden  23
irrigation line  10
jasper  37
Kakadu National Park  7, 27
Kalbarri National Park  24
Kalgoorlie  24
kangaroo  11, 47, 61
Kangaroo Island  21
Kangaroo Paw, Red and Green  22
Kata Tjuta  29
Kimberley ranges  48
Kings Park, Perth  22
Koala  30
Lake Burley Griffin  34, 35
Lakes in western Tasmania  18
Lamington National Park  31
Launceston  16
lichen  41
Lionfish  47
Litchfield National Park  27

lizard, dragon  45
Lorikeet, Scaly-breasted  43
Lyrebird, Superb  4
MacDonnell Ranges  28
Mallee Fowl  15
Melbourne Cricket Ground  12
Mindil Beach  26
mountains  37, 39
Mt Arapiles  15
Mt Augustus  22
Mt Bogong  14
Murray River  14, 20
   paddlesteamer  14
Nambung National Park  24
Nargun, Den of  13
Narooma  11
National Gallery of Australia  36
National Science & Technology Centre  36
National Soldiers War Memorial  52, 63
Nature's Window  24
Ned Kelly armour  51, 63
Ochre Pits  28
opal  21
Orchid, Cooktown  30
Organ Pipes  39
outback river  4
Pandani  18
Parliament House, Brisbane  4
   Canberra  35, 59
Parrot, Australian King  2, 3
   Australian Ringneck  2, 3
Pebbly Beach  11
Penguin, Little  13
Perth  22, 57
   Town Hall  51
Pilbara mine  53
Pine, Bunya  42
Pinnacles  24
plant roots  38, 41
plants, flowering  42, 61
Platypus  8
plunge pool  38
polyps, zoanthid  45
Port Adelaide  20
Possum, Leadbeater's  14
Puffing Billy  13
Purnululu National Park  25
rainforest  33
   subtropical  31
Red Centre  26
Remarkable Rocks  21
Richmond Bridge  17, 56

rock art, Aboriginal  27
Scarborough Beach  22
sea cucumber  49
Sea-lion, Australian  21
seaweed  42
Shark Bay  24, 48
shrub  41
Silverton Hotel  10
Skyrail gondola  33
Snake, Tiger  46
South Bank Beach  30, 58
   Parklands  30, 58
spider  44
   web  44
stromatolites  48
Sturt's Desert Pea  19
   Desert Rose  26
sundews  43
Surf Lifesaving Carnival  7
Sydney  50
   Harbour Bridge  9
   Opera House  8, 50, 54
Telstra Tower  36
Termite mounds, Magnetic  27
Three Sisters  9
Top End bushland  49
Torrens River  19, 56
Treetop Walk  23
trepang  49
Trinity Inlet  33
Tully River  32
turbine, Snowy River  11
Twelve Apostles  15
Ubirr, NT  7
Uluru  29, 58
Valley of the Giants  23
vineyard, SA  19
volcanic plug  37
Waratah  8
Warrumbungles  39
Wattle, Golden  5
Wave Rock  23
Westgate Bridge  13
Whaling Museum  23
Whitehaven Beach  32
whitewater rafting  32
Whitsunday Islands  32, 59
Wilpena Pound  20
Wineglass Bay  17
Wollongong  11
Wombat, Southern Hairy-nosed  19
Zebra  10
Zuytdorp Cliffs  50

First published by Steve Parish Publishing Pty Ltd
PO Box 1058, Archerfield, Queensland 4108, Australia
**www.steveparish.com.au**
© copyright Steve Parish Publishing Pty Ltd, 2001
Discover and Learn about Australia is a trademark of Steve Parish Publishing Pty Ltd
Printed in Singapore.
Colour separations by Inprint Pty Ltd, Brisbane, Queensland, Australia.
ISBN 1 74021 058 1

**Photography: Steve Parish**
Additional photography: Pat Slater, crocodile, p. 27, kangaroo, p. 47; Belinda Wright, Aboriginal man, p. 48, fire, p. 49; Leanne Nobilio, baby girl (Allegra Nobilio), p. 53.

Text design and assembly: Leanne Nobilio, Nobilio Design, Brisbane
Cover design: Leanne Staff, SPP

**Text: Pat Slater**